Howard Pickersgill

W9-CAP-597

Great Paintings

CHARTWELL BOOKS INC.

Designed and produced by
Albany Books
36 Park Street London W1Y 4DE

First published 1979

Published by Chartwell Books Inc.
A Division of Book Sales Inc.
110 Enterprise Avenue
Secaucus, New Jersey 07094

Copyright © Albany Books 1979

Printed in Hong Kong

All rights reserved. No part of this
publication may be reproduced, stored
in a retrieval system or transmitted in
any form or by any means, electronic,
mechanical, photocopying, recording or
otherwise, without the prior permission
of the copyright owner

Design: Jill Della Casa
Picture research: Mary Corcoran

Acknowledgements

Cliches Musées Nationaux, Paris: pages 58/9, 94/5,
100/1, 114/5.

The Cooper-Bridgeman Library, London: 4, 34/5,
36/7, 48/9, 68/9, 72/3, 78/9, 84/5, 86/7, 92/3, 98/9.
102/3, 104/5, 120/1, endpapers.

The Courtauld Institute Galleries, London: 106/7,
116/7.

The Metropolitan Museum of Art, New York (Bequest
of Mrs H. O. Havemeyer, 1929. The Havemeyer
Collection): 50/1, 110/1.

The Trustees of The National Gallery, London: 6/7,
13, 14/5, 18/9, 22/3, 24/5, 32/3, 40/1, 46/7, 52/3,
62/3, 66/7, 70/1, 74/5, 76/7, 80/1, 90/1, 122/3.

Scala, Florence: 8/9, 10/1, 16/7, 20/1, 26/7, 28/9,
30/1, 38/9, 42/3, 56/7, 60/1, 64/5, 96/7, 108/9,
112/3.

The Tate Gallery, London: 88/9, 119, 125
(© SPADEM, Paris 1979)

The Walker Art Gallery, Liverpool: 44/5.

The Trustees of The Wallace Collection, London:
front jacket, 54/5, 82/3.

**Page 4: *Rembrandt* Titus, the Artist's
Son** *(By courtesy of Christie's)*

**Opposite: *Turner* 'The Fighting
Téméraire'** *detail (National Gallery,
London)*

4

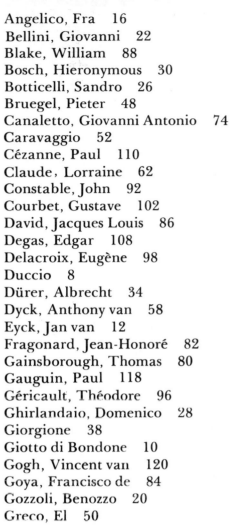

The Painters

Duccio   c.1255/60-1318/9

Few details are known of the life of Duccio. He is described as being 'active' between 1278 and 1319 and was the leading painter in Siena at that time.

Unlike his contemporary, the Florentine Giotto, Duccio was not a revolutionary in either the pictorial or the technical sense. His work does, however, mark a transition from Byzantine art to the Early Renaissance. This period began the development of western European art as we now know it and was based on the rediscovery of the art of classical Greece and Rome. In Duccio's work the Byzantine influence is retained in the use of gilding as the background to the events depicted; and in the emphasis he still places upon the use of pictorial art as part of religious ritual.

There is evidence that Duccio was also influenced by Gothic art which, in the form of miniatures and book illuminations, was spreading into Italy from the north and west of Europe. This art was less formalised and ritualistic and more realistic.

In 1308 he was commissioned to produce his greatest work, the *Maestà* for the high altar of the cathedral in Siena. One side of the work is filled with a picture of the Virgin and child throned in majesty and surrounded by angels and saints. On the other side are forty-four pictures showing scenes from the life of Christ. These reveal Duccio as a master of the narrative or story-telling picture. The scenes are lively in action, acute in observation, splendidly composed and sensuously rich in colour. A sign of the new Gothic influence can be seen in the way in which Duccio uses the faces of the figures in these pictures to convey the emotion of the scene.

When the work was completed in 1311 it was carried in triumph from Duccio's studio, through the crowded streets of Siena, to the cathedral. This was a proud day for citizens and artist alike. The work is huge and painted on both sides of wooden panels. Thanks to modern technology the two sides have been separated and can be seen in the cathedral museum under carefully controlled light and temperature conditions.

Rucellai Madonna
(Uffizi Gallery, Florence)

This picture, which is about 15ft (4.6m) high, now stands in the Uffizi Gallery in Florence dramatically flanked by similar-sized Madonnas by Duccio's great Florentine contemporaries, Cimabue and Giotto. It originally hung in the Rucellai family's private chapel in the church of Sta. Maria Novella in Florence. It was at one time thought to be the work of Cimabue but the more lyrical rhythms and the greater realism of the enthroned Madonna and child leave little doubt that it is the work of Duccio. The individualism expressed in the faces of Madonna, child and angels recalls the northern or Gothic influence, as does the drapery behind the seated figure. The throne shows the beginnings of the understanding of architectural perspective in painting.

9

Giotto di Bondone
c.1267-1337

Giotto was born about 1267 and although his fame was widespread in his own lifetime little is known about his life. It is known that he owned a house in Florence in 1305, that he joined the painters' guild in Florence in 1311 and that he was in Florence again between 1318 and 1320. Between 1329 and 1333 he worked in Naples as court painter to Robert of Anjou — he painted many murals for the king's private rooms and chapel but hardly a trace of these works remains.

In 1334 Giotto was appointed 'capomaestro' to the cathedral at Florence and put in charge of the city's fortifications. In that year the foundations for the cathedral's bell-tower were laid. This campanile, usually referred to as 'Giotto's Tower', was certainly designed by him but by the time of his death in 1337 only the two lower courses had been built; the design of the tower was then altered and completed by other artists.

Giotto was the forerunner of the Renaissance ideal, the 'universal man' of many capacities and achievements. Besides being a painter, Giotto was also sculptor and architect. He designed the Carraia bridge in Florence in addition to his work on the city's fortifications and the cathedral campanile. According to Boccaccio he was 'good-natured, witty, shrewd and the greatest painter since antiquity'.

Not all the works attributed to Giotto can be authenticated. There are unspecified works in the church of S. Francesco, Assissi. He painted a crucifix for the church of Sta. Maria Novella in Florence. Of the frescoes in the Bardi and the Peruzzi chapels in the church of S. Croce in Florence, those in the latter are thought to be more reliably his handiwork.

The frescoes in the Scrovegni family oratory in the Arena Chapel in Padua are unquestionably by Giotto. They were painted when he was at the height of his powers and are considered to be his finest work. *The Flight into Egypt* shown opposite is a detail from this chapel. *Ognissanti Madonna,* from the church of Ognissanti in Florence, is attributed to his middle years because of its similarity of style and treatment to his work in Padua.

Giotto broke away from the copying of mediaeval formulae and he considerably extended pictorial representation by dropping the use of gilded backgrounds in favour of direct observation of nature. The influence of the sculptors Arnolfo di Cambio and Pisano, who had earlier reacted against past techniques and attitudes, and his own sculptural interests gave his figures greater volume.

Like Duccio, Giotto is a great story-teller in pictorial form but his stories are concerned with moral weight rather than with divine splendour.

The Flight into Egypt
(Arena Chapel, Padua)

The most noticeable thing about this picture is the landscape setting and blue sky which replace a gilded background. The landscape is stated simply but this simplicity could be deliberate so as to concentrate attention on the central story of the picture. The drawing of the figures and the donkey suggest real understanding of their forms and of spatial relationships. The faces of the figures are individual and expressive, as are their movements and the gestures of the hands. The colour is warm and tender whilst expressing the artist's cool scientific detachment.

Jan van Eyck c.1390-1441

Jan van Eyck was the more significant of two brothers, Jan and Hubert, who were both painters. They sometimes worked together and an example of this cooperation is the large composition entitled *Adoration of the Lamb*.

In 1422 van Eyck entered the service of John of Bavaria, Count of Holland. Three years later he was appointed Court Painter to Philip the Good, Duke of Burgundy. In addition to his duties as Court Painter, Jan was used by the Duke on secret diplomatic missions to Spain and Portugal. In 1430 he moved to Bruges and lived there until his death in 1441. He painted many religious subjects as well as a great number of portraits. *The Marriage of Giovanni Arnolfini and Giovanna Cenami*, shown opposite, is without doubt his most widely known portrait.

His work exhibits extraordinary technical control and facility and represents a high-water mark in realistic painting. He had great feeling for contrasting textures and responded with quick and sensitive understanding to light effects and spatial relationships. European painters became increasingly preoccupied with light and space and northern painters such as van Eyck played an important part in the development of their understanding and interpretation into colour. Observing, selecting and visually recording all the subtleties of real life, he makes his statements clearly and objectively.

It is possible that the particular qualities displayed in van Eyck's work would have been impossible to achieve without the use of a mixture of oil and pigment. Indeed, he is often credited with discovering the values of linseed oil in painting — but 'discovering' is a word to be viewed with caution in this context. It is safe to say that he played an important part in the development and adoption of its use. All pigment needs a 'medium' so that it can be applied as a wash or paste to the picture surface. Up until this time, the commonest medium had been egg tempera in which the yolk is used to bind the pigment. Egg tempera has the advantage of giving vital glowing colour; it has the disadvantage of drying very hard and very quickly so that alterations, wiping-off or over-painting are all difficult. Linseed oil on the other hand dries slowly and leaves the paint plastic and flexible for quite a long time. The use of this medium was taken to Italy by Antonella da Messina but its adoption there was much slower than in northern Europe.

Jan van Eyck acquired considerable fame throughout Europe in the fifteenth century and his works were eagerly collected in Renaissance Italy.

The Marriage of Giovanni Arnolfini and Giovanna Cenami
(National Gallery, London)

This picture would probably have been impossible to achieve through any medium other than oil painting. In that sense alone, it represents a significant step forward in the history of painting. It also makes an important contribution to portrait painting in general and to group portraiture in particular.

All of van Eyck's observational powers are revealed here and the discarded shoes on the floor and oranges on the table give a sense of realism to the painting. The convex mirror gives a picture within the picture, a reflection of the witnesses to the wedding ceremony. One of these was probably van Eyck himself as he has written over the mirror the words 'Jan van Eyck was here'. The use of the dog at the feet of the couple, and of their hands lightly held together, simply and effectively bonds the pair in their betrothal; at the same time it unifies the composition.

Paolo Uccello
1397-1475

Paolo Uccello, craftsman, painter and worker in mosaics, was born in Florence in 1397. Part of his training and experience was gained in the workshops of Ghiberti the designer and executor of the famous Baptistery doors in Florence, the last pair of which were later described by Michelangelo as 'worthy to form the Gates of Paradise'. Uccello could hardly have experienced a stronger or better influence and it was a highly stimulating and formative period of his life. He was with Ghiberti from 1407 to 1415 and then worked for a short time in Venice.

Uccello was essentially a man of the Renaissance, concerned to break away from the International Gothic style. Throughout his life he was preoccupied with the exciting problems of perspective and with geometrical structures underlying the pictorial composition. There are two kinds of perspective: linear or architectural, in which lines are used to suggest spatial relationships and recession on the two-dimensional picture surface; and aerial, in which colour is used. Uccello's concern was chiefly with linear perspective and it is his work in this field that ensures him an important place in the development of western European painting.

The murals painted by Uccello in the cloister of Sta. Maria Novella in

> ### Battle of San Romano
> *(National Gallery, London)*
>
> *Depicting the rout from a series of three paintings, this picture suggests some of the qualities of a stage setting with the foreground figures and horses on the platform of the stage and behind it a backcloth of landscape with fleeing and fighting figures. Closer investigation makes it evident that the figures have volume and movement, though the movement of the horses is only imperfectly understood which adds to the slightly theatrical appearance. The most exciting feature of the picture is the use of lances, swords and the trimmings of the horses. These weld the compositional design firmly together at the same time as suggesting spatial recession.*

Florence show him at his best and clearest. *Flood* particularly demonstrates his understanding of the structural principles of perspective, compositional design and human anatomy which were worked out by Brunelleschi, the great architect of the cathedral in Florence, the sculptor Donatello and the painter Masaccio.

There are three versions of *Battle of San Romano*, the one depicted hanging in London. The others are in Paris and Florence. They were painted about five years later than the murals in Sta. Maria Novella and have an abstract patterning which may owe something to the tapestries executed by north European artists for the Medici palaces. Uccello's equestrian portrait of the English mercenary Sir John Hawkwood (Giovanni Acuto to the Italians), and the painted clock with four heads in the Duomo in Florence, further demonstrates his powers.

Uccello applied principles which were already clearly understood, defined and applied in the three-dimensional arts of architecture and sculpture to the two-dimensional art of painting. In addition he achieved a plastic quality in the handling of paint which was hardly equalled in his lifetime.

Fra Angelico
c.1400-1455

Fra Angelico, also known as Beato Angelico, began his artistic career as a miniaturist in the school of Lorenzo Monaco. He took his vows as a monk in the Dominican Order in 1408 at Fiesole. The Dominican Order discouraged individualism in the artist in favour of the use of art as the servant of religion.

Fra Angelico was a highly professional artist and it is obvious from his work that he gained much stimulus from the Florentine artists of his day. Evidence of this can be seen in the *Crucifixion* he painted for the Dominican convent in Fiesole. It is directly based on *Trinity* painted by Masaccio for the church of Sta. Maria Novella in Florence.

Annunciation
(Convent of S. Marco, Florence)

The most striking feature of this picture is its glowing colour, particularly the carmine pink of the gown worn by the Archangel. The minutely observed detail in the Archangel's wings and the wild flowers outside the building also strikes the eye.

The composition is effectively held together by carefully drawn architectural detail. Religious pictures of specific events such as the Annunciation acquire traditions or conventions. This one is unusual in that the white lily, the symbol of chastity, is not included in the picture.

The architectural setting in *Annunciation* shown here is directly related to the work of the contemporary architect Michelozzo who was a pupil of Brunelleschi, the great designer of the cathedral of Florence. In Angelico's fresco *Scenes from the lives of SS. Stephen and Lawrence,* which he painted for the private chapel of Pope Nicholas V in the Vatican, there is a strong emphasis on story-telling from observation. This, coupled with his use of space and the solidity of his figures, brings him very much into line with the mainstream of 15th-century fresco painting. Indeed there are strong affinities in his work with that of Piero della Francesca.

The fact that Fra Angelico did not always identify himself with the more advanced contemporary ideas, and that he sometimes used compositional designs and pictorial motifs from the past, is doubtless partly due to the teaching of the Dominicans; it also represents deliberate personal choice.

Perhaps Angelico's best known work is the series of frescoes in the convent of S. Marco in Florence. This convent had been rebuilt by Michelozzo between 1438 and 1445 at the order of Cosimo Medici. The frescoes were painted with the assistance of other monks between 1438 and 1447. In spiritual terms the frescoes are intended as a guide to, and expression of, the religious life and disciplined devotion of the Dominican community. In artistic terms they demonstrate great economy in drawing and composition; a freshness and clarity of colour and a quality which places them beyond conventional time and space.

Fra Angelico died on a visit to the convent of Sta. Maria supra Minerva in Rome and was buried there. John Ruskin, the 19th-century English art critic, described him as 'not an artist properly so-called but an inspired saint'. This had been the prevailing opinion from the 16th to the 19th centuries and the Pre-Raphaelites admired him but thought his work 'primitive'. His true worth and his valuable contribution are now appreciated more strongly.

Piero della Francesca
c. 1420-1492

Piero della Francesca was born in Borgo San Sepolcro, a small town in Umbria. He was devoted to his home town and throughout his life spent as much time there as he could although his work took him to Ferrara, Rimini, Arezzo, Rome and Urbino. The origins of his style are essentially Florentine and he painted frescoes in the church of S. Egidio in Florence with Domenico Veneziano in 1439. His *Madonna della Misericordia* painted in 1445 shows that he had studied and assimilated the artistic ideas of Masaccio, Donatello, Uccello and other Florentine artists.

Piero's contribution was to present their range of ideas with a new refinement and unity. The figures in his paintings give such a sense of volume and solidity that they appear as inevitable extensions to the pictorial setting. He was exceptional in expressing the fine balance between the artificial and the natural, and between the sophisticated and the rural. This is achieved by careful precision in the drawing of outlines and sublety in the use of light. His artistic imagination demanded clarity, dignity and orderliness — both in thought and in pictorial interpretation.

These attributes are evident in all of Piero's works but especially so in *The Tribute Money* and in his great narrative fresco, *The Story of the True Cross*, in the choir of the church of S. Francesco in Arezzo. He used geometrical relationships of shape and perspective not merely to create a pattern on the surface of the picture, as is sometimes felt of Uccello, but as the real foundation of spatial effect.

Piero della Francesca is now considered one of the greatest and most intellectual of the galaxy of painters of the Early Renaissance in Italy. It is surprising therefore that his work went through a long period of obscurity and was virtually overlooked until the middle of the last century. 20th-century artists highly respect the control and discipline of his drawing, colour and compositional design which is always accompanied by warmth and feeling.

Baptism
(National Gallery, London)

This was one of Piero's first commissions after his return to his home town of Borgo San Sepolcro in 1442. The little town is depicted as a background to the figures. The man who is pulling his shirt over his head, with the form of the body clearly implied inside the cloth, indicates the precision of Piero's drawing and his observational powers. The colour is coolly dispassionate but not unfeeling. The composition is built up on a series of verticals — the figures and the trees; horizontals — the clouds, the dove and the terracing on the hills; and on a series of related arcs — the tree and its foliage, the figures of Christ and John the Baptist and the figure with the shirt — which are all related to the arched framework of the picture.

18

Benozzo Gozzoli
c.1421-1497

Benozzo Gozzoli, a Florentine, was apprenticed to a goldsmith and in the early years of his career worked with Ghiberti on the doors for the Baptistery in Florence, as did Uccello. He also worked with Fra Angelico in Rome and Orvieto. This was a time of seething curiosity and exciting discoveries and many of the great painters of the time worked together.

Gozzoli's experience was obviously wide and his facility considerable, but he was not a very original thinker and his work was primarily decorative. The word 'decorative', as applied to an artist, has become a derogatory term in the 20th century but it would not be fair to dismiss Gozzoli thus summarily. His craftsmanship, technical mastery and sensitive observational powers were all of a high order. It was apt that Piero de Medici chose him to decorate the chapel in his palace. Both patron and artist shared a taste for pageantry and the rich Burgundian tapestries being imported into Italy at this time influenced each of them.

From this fortunate combination of personalities comes *Journey of the Magi*, perhaps the most glittering fresco of the century. It may owe some debt to Gentile da Fabriano's *Adoration of the Magi* but the fresco stands in its own right as a remarkable achievement. The chapel which it adorns is small and square with an altar recess and the four walls of the chamber are covered with the fresco.

The main characters are portraits of members of the Medici family, a revealing example of self-aggrandisement. The landscape and architecture through which the characters journey are as changelessly Tuscan as can be imagined. To stand in the small confined space of this chapel, surrounded by these frescoes, is an absorbing and unique experience.

Another major work by Gozzoli is a fresco-cycle of scenes from the Old Testament commissioned for the Campo Santo in Pisa in 1467. Unhappily this is now badly damaged. An altarpiece is in the National Gallery, London and a painting of S. Sebastian is in San Gemignano in Tuscany. Apart from these, there seems to be little known or left of his work.

Journey of the Magi
(Chapel of the Palazzo Medici-Riccardi, Florence)

The main figure in this painting is a portrait of Lorenzo de' Medici and the figure following from the left is that of Gozzoli's patron, Piero de Medici. Such arrogance must have been frowned upon by the church. Gozzoli's drawing of the figures is full of searching and individual observation and their sumptuous apparel is clearly described. The background, though a little theatrical and not quite in scale, is alive with the vitality of action and nature.

Giovanni Bellini
c. 1430-1516

Giovanni Bellini was one of a family of painters with a flourishing studio workshop. Jacopo was the father, Gentile and Giovanni the sons. In addition, they had a close working relationship with Giovanni's brother-in-law, Andrea Mantegna.

Giovanni, sometimes called Giambellini, was the most significant artist of the Bellini trio. He was trained largely by his father but the strongest influence upon the development of his mature style came from Mantegna. This influence can be seen by a comparison of their individual versions of *The Agony in the Garden*. Both pictures were painted in 1465 and the compositional design and figure drawing in each have strong similarities. Their landscapes are treated in very different ways and Bellini's version gives evidence of a more direct observation of light, colour and spatial recession.

Bellini was highly responsive to nature in all her hours and seasons but, unlike the work of Florentine artists, the mood of his pictures is contemplative rather than active. *Madonna with Saints*, which Giovanni painted for the Frari church in Venice, finally breaks away from Mantegna's influence. The picture is characteristic of the Venetian School of painting in its early stages.

In 1479 Bellini was appointed chief painter to the Republic of Venice, holding this position until his death in 1516. His work included portraits of the Doges and the one reproduced opposite is considered the finest.

Bellini was probably the most inventive painter produced by northern Italy, assimilating influences from several sources and expressing them in a new form of pictorial expression; this in turn created strong influences for later generations. From this time the Venetian School begins to be a recognisable entity in its own right with the understanding of colour and light and their translation into paint being the primary concern of the Venetian artist. Venice was transformed from an artistically provincial city into a fully fledged Renaissance centre comparable with Florence and Rome.

Doge Leonardo Loredan
(National Gallery, London)

In this portrait Bellini borrows from the Flemish painters by adopting the three-quarter view. The simplicity of the composition is probably the picture's most striking attribute. The rectangular shape at the base of the picture supports the pyramid-like chest and shoulders which then give support to the head. The background is not allowed to distract from the figure itself. The richness of colour and texture is notable and the subtlety of light playing upon the modelling of the head gives a sculptural quality to the figure.

This portrait is one of the first in which oil paint is used in an 'impasto' technique, when the pigment is applied thickly with the brush strokes clearly showing. The technqiue, unusual in the 15th century, has been very widely used since the time of the Impressionists.

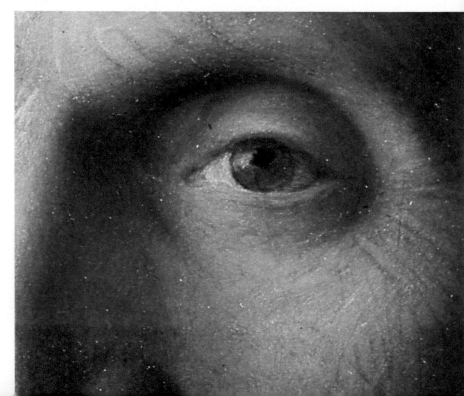

IOANNES BELLINVS

23

Andrea Mantegna
c.1431-1506

Andrea Mantegna spent the first twelve years of his life in Padua. The sculptor Donatello was active in Padua in the 1440s and his influence is apparent in much of Mantegna's work. He married Giovanni Bellini's sister and although one year younger, his ideas exerted a strong influence upon Giovanni. In 1460 Mantegna was appointed court painter in Mantua, a city which was establishing itself as one of the leading centres of the new humanist philosophy. While in Mantua he produced many paintings for, and portraits of, the ruling family, the Gonzagas. In 1484 Francesco Gonzaga commissioned *The Triumph of Caesar* which consists of nine canvases, each 9ft (2.75m) square. They were subsequently bought by Charles I of England and are now housed in the Orangery at Hampton Court Palace.

Mantegna's style is distinguished by the three-dimensional qualities of his figures. The modelling of form in the description of figures or landscape is architectural in feeling. It is helpful to recall that during the period of the Renaissance — the re-discovery of the glories of the art of classical Greece and Rome — there were many classical remains in northern Italy and Mantegna would have been very conscious of them. This awareness, and his early contact with the humanist movement, developed in his work a scholarly accuracy of architectural and archaeological detail as well as an austerity of feeling. The expression of personal emotion is strictly controlled and his drawing shows a mastery in the foreshortening of the human figure which was unequalled in his lifetime. All these abilities are clearly seen in *The Agony in the Garden*.

Mantegna was one of the few painters of the 15th century whose fame and influence never declined. Artists such as Albrecht Dürer, at the end of the 15th century, and Nicholas Poussin during the 17th century, admired his expression of classical ideas in the terms of the Renaissance. Their paintings indicate the lasting importance of Mantegna by the way in which they adapted his ideas to their own.

The Agony in the Garden
(National Gallery, London)

The foreground figures of the sleeping disciples immediately point to Mantegna's masterly drawing of foreshortened figures. The city in the middle distance demonstrates his knowledge of, and interest in, the architecture of classical antiquity — the compositional balance is as satisfying as a masterpiece of architectural design, despite the slightly artificial quality of the landscape. The mood of the picture is quietly appropriate to its subject matter. The approaching group of people and soldiers remain a distant, and not immediate, threat.

Sandro Botticelli
c.1446-1510

Little is known of Botticelli's youth, except that he was born in Florence. It is likely that he worked under the artist Filippo Lippi and that he was influenced by Verocchio, the pupil of Donatello and teacher of Leonardo da Vinci.

It would seem that Lorenzo di Pierfrancesco de Medici, second cousin to Lorenzo (Il Magnifico) de Medici, commissioned the two mythological and allegorical paintings *Primavera* and *Birth of Venus*. These are visual expressions of the current philosophy that 'Beauty is the visible token of the Divine'. Such philosophy denotes a definite breakaway from the 'sacred' as being the only proper and acceptable subject matter for the pictorial artist. It also represents a decided and permanent shift in patronage from the church to the men of power, education and riches.

Botticelli may have come under the influence of Savonarola, the Florentine Dominican preacher and reformer. It was once thought that this caused him to repent of his pagan or secular pictures

Birth of Venus
(Uffizi, Florence)

This picture represents an unreal world of delightful fantasy and insubstantiality, wherein lies much of its charm. The grace and stylized formality of the figures, waves and flowers are deliberately designed to feed the mystery and imagination of the beholder. Underlying all this is the true Renaissance artist who is concerned with the techniques of pure line, luminous colour and the visual expression of the relationship between form and space.

and that he stopped painting altogether; the former is doubtful and the latter is quite untrue. Certainly his work became more intense and in the latter part of his life he belonged to a group of artists who reacted against the scientific and naturalistic ideas propounded by Masaccio and other early Renaissance painters in Italy. He tried to revive some of the earlier Gothic ideas in his own work which resulted in an ornamental use of line, giving a delicacy of touch which veered towards the sentimental.

Mystic Nativity, painted by Botticelli in 1500, belongs to this later period of his work. It includes an inscription from the Apocalypse which seems to imply Botticelli's expectation of the end of the world. The real meaning of the picture has never been understood but perhaps the year of its production might offer some form of explanation — in 1000 and again in 1500 people had anticipated divine intervention in the affairs of mankind.

In his own day, Botticelli's reputation was rather limited and he died in obscurity in 1510. His fame was resurrected in the 19th century by the Pre-Raphaelites, who attempted to imitate his elongated figures, and by John Ruskin, the eminent art critic and historian. An unexpected offshoot of this awakened interest in Botticelli's work was the contributory influence it exerted upon the movement at the turn of the 19th and 20th centuries known as Art Nouveau.

Domenico Ghirlandaio 1449-1494

Domenico Ghirlandaio's real name was Domenico di Tommaso Bigordi. He was born in Florence in 1449 and was styled 'Il Ghirlandaio', the garland-maker, after his father who was a goldsmith.

He eventually established a flourishing workshop in Florence with his two brothers and Michelangelo spent a short period in his studios, a period probably more formative and influential for Michelangelo than was ever admitted. Ghirlandaio was one of the most accomplished fresco painters of the later 15th century and a master of the narrative picture. He himself studied under Baldovinetti and his style was influenced by the work of Castagno, Filippo Lippi, Masaccio and Verocchio. He received many commissions, but few came from cultured and aristocratic patrons and, most notably perhaps, none at all from the Medici family. This was because, though technically highly competent, his work tended to popularise well-established pictorial methods and was probably considered old-fashioned by the more 'cultured'.

His methods did appeal to the rising middle-classes and his habit of incorporating portraits of his contemporaries into religious frescoes assured him a steady patronage. *Christ calling the First Apostles* in the Sistine Chapel included portraits of many Florentines living in Rome at the time and this almost certainly secured him the commission for the fresco *Scenes from the Life of St. Francis* from Francesco Sassetti, painted between 1482 and 1485 in the family chapel in the church of Sta. Trinità in Florence.

His largest commission was the fresco cycle in the choir of Sta. Maria Novella in Florence, illustrating *Scenes from the Life of the Virgin and St. John the Baptist* which was painted between 1486 and 1490. It was commissioned by Giovanni Tornabuoni, a partner in the Medici banking enterprise, and the story is pictured as though the events had taken place in the home of a wealthy Florentine merchant.

Ghirlandaio had great talent for portraying the life and style of his time. He had great skill in the management of complex compositional designs and was a considerable craftsman. In addition, he was sensitively alive to the realism of the Flemish painters and had a genuine feeling for the factual in nature. He died in Florence in 1494, aged only 45.

Old Man and Boy
(Louvre, Paris)

There is great tenderness as well as honesty of observation in this double portrait. Ghirlandaio does not avoid the disfigured nose of the old man and, in doing so, incorporates it easily into the beauty and harmony of the picture as a whole. The landscape seen through the window is a delightful picture in itself and also gives clear evidence of Ghirlandaio's interest in the direct observation of nature.

29

Hieronymous Bosch
c.1450-1516

Bosch's name comes from his native town of s'Hertogenbosch in the Netherlands. Born the son of a minor painter he was, throughout his life, a highly individual figure both in personal character and in artistic expression. In 1480 he completed the panels for the church of St. John in his home town which had been left unfinished by his father. Several paintings by him remained in this church well into the 17th century. During the 1480s he inherited property and married into a comparatively rich family. The fact that he did not have to

---

Hell from *Garden of Delights*
(Prado, Madrid)

Hell is the right wing of a triptych. The left wing represents the Creation and the Garden of Eden; the central and largest panel depicts the delights and follies of life in between the two. Reading this panel from bottom to top the spectator appears to be taken on a journey from the limitations of mortality across the river of death, a strange and unexpected classical allusion, to the conventional burning and disintegration of life which fits with a more mediaeval concept of hell. In bringing together the classical and mediaeval references in this way, Bosch would appear to have been at least aware of the spirit of the Renaissance despite his exceptional individuality of outlook.

rely on his painting as a means of living may partly explain the individuality of his pictorial expression.

The origins of his style are obscure. His works seem to have nothing in common with that of Rogier van der Weyden or Jan van Eyck, the two most influential painters of his time in the Netherlands. Nevertheless, from whatever source or by whatever means, he developed a superb painting technique with glowing but finely controlled colour. The most outstanding aspect of his work is his obvious delight in landscape, shown by the prominence it has in all his works.

Bosch was an orthodox Catholic and a prominent member of a local religious brotherhood. In spite of the lack of convention in his work, he enjoyed the patronage of Catholic bodies and of Philip II of Spain. His reputation was high throughout his lifetime and continued so after his death in 1516.

There are about forty authenticated works by Bosch still in existence. The majority of them have strong elements of fantasy with half-human, half-animal figures; strange creatures and demons jumbled with recognisable humans and set in scenes of imaginary landscape and architecture. The basic theme seems to be constant; the folly of the human species and the terrible consequences of its sins. The *Garden of Delights* triptych, one panel of which is shown opposite, is probably his best known work.

Bosch's pictorial fantasy has had a strong attraction for artists in the 20th century. The Surrealists proudly claimed him as one of the more important of their artistic ancestors but several attempts in this century to find a psychological explanation for his imagery have all been inconclusive.

Leonardo da Vinci 1452-1519

Leonardo da Vinci was born in Anchiano, a village near the town of Vinci in Tuscany, the illegitimate son of a Florentine notary and a peasant girl called Caterina. Little is known of his youth and upbringing, but he was enrolled as a painter in the Fraternity of St. Luke in Florence in 1472 and was at this time a pupil of Verrocchio.

He remained in Florence for the next decade and his greatest work of this period is his *Adoration of the Kings,* commissioned for the church of S. Donato a Scoperto in 1481. Very little of this work is developed beyond the ground painting and, like so much of his painting, it has remained unfinished.

Work on it was doubtless interrupted when he went to Milan in 1482 where he was recommended to Lodovico Il Moro as a musician. He remained there until the French conquest of Milan in 1499. His greatest works of the Milan period were the *Sforza Monument* which was never completed and is known only from drawings; the famous mural *The Last Supper* in the refectory of the convent of Sta. Maria delle Grazie; and the two versions of *The Virgin of the Rocks* upon which he worked for some twenty years.

Between 1500 and 1506 Leonardo was back in Florence working on the cartoon for the fresco of *The Battle of Anghiari* which was commissioned by the Signoria for the Council Chamber of the Palazzo Vecchio but unfortunately destroyed in 1565. During this time he also painted the *Mona Lisa* — perhaps the most famous picture in the world — and the cartoon for the theme *Virgin and Child with St. Anne and the Infant St. John.* The picture *Leda and the Swan,* known only from an existing copy and strangely different from the devotional sensitivity and perception of *The Last Supper,* is also thought to belong to this period.

Leonardo returned to Milan in 1506 and was appointed Painter and Engineer to Francis I of France. He was invited to live in the Château of Cloux, near Amboise on the Loire, in 1517 and died there two years later.

It has been said of Leonardo that his paintings were seldom finished because he felt that they would never match up to his own high standards. When he went to Milan he described himself as an 'artificer of instruments of war' and certainly from that time applied-science occupied much of his time; his notebooks were filled with studies of structures and movements in birds, skeletons, flowers, water and human embryos. He was forever searching but his discoveries were never systematically formulated and most of his theories were found faulty when put into practice.

Leonardo is considered one of the two greatest artists of the Renaissance. Living in an age when art and science were not considered separate, but as two branches of 'knowledge', Leonardo lived up to the Renaissance ideal of 'the universal man'.

The Virgin of the Rocks
(National Gallery, London)

The three-dimensional pyramidal basis of the figures implied in this picture is its outstanding compositional quality. The landscape background demonstrates Leonardo's interest in the geological structure of rocks and mountains and the Sfumato (smoke) technique, whereby outlines are softened and colour is graded imperceptibly from one shade to another, is considered to be one of Leonardo's greatest contributions to the development of European painting.

Albrecht Dürer 1471-1528

Albrecht Dürer was the son of a gold-smith in Nuremburg and the godson of Anthony Koberger, one of Germany's foremost printers and publishers of the time. At the age of fifteen he was apprenticed to Michael Wolgemut, one of the leading painters and book illustrators of northern Europe. These early influences from the graphic arts, and the devotion to meticulous detail which is the hallmark of the goldsmith's work, show in all of Dürer's own work. Moreover, thanks to the influence of these men of standing and reputation, his ambitions reached out well beyond the normal studio workshop training of the time.

In 1490, after his apprenticeship, he travelled through northern Europe and journeyed to Colmar in order to meet and learn from the great painter and engraver Martin Schongauer. Unfortunately Schongauer died before Dürer reached Colmar. He then worked for a time as an illustrator in Basel before returning to Nuremburg in 1494. In the same year he married and, after a short visit to northern Italy, he set up a studio workshop in his native town.

Throughout his working career Dürer was equally active as painter, engraver and wood-cutter and his technical facility in all of these areas developed constantly and considerably. His work was continually in demand and he received commissions from many sources. From 1512 onwards his most important patron was the Holy Roman Emperor Maximilian.

Dürer's work reflected the living spirit of the Reformation in northern Europe and that of the Italian Renaissance from the south. He delighted in the problems of perspective and in the classical ideals of proportion, harmony and balance. He particularly admired the work of the Venetian painters, Bellini and Mantegna, an influence which enriched and extended his use of colour. His personal delight in the observation of nature is evident in the landscapes incorporated into his pictures. This interest in landscape was to become a recurrent and increasing aspect of the contribution made by northern artists to western European art in general, culminating in its firm establishment as an art form in its own right by French painters, particularly the Impressionists, in the 19th century.

At his death in 1528 Dürer was widely known and respected as a painter, but his chief fame rested for several centuries upon his work as an engraver, his printed works being used throughout Europe almost as we now use text-books.

Self-portrait 1498
(Prado, Madrid)

Dürer painted several self-portraits for which reason he is sometimes dubbed 'narcissistic'. He was obviously intrigued by the many facets of his own complex personality and, by the depiction of himself in different guises, he projected these facets into images which he could study. An aspect of this process included a fondness for 'dressing-up' and in one portrait he dressed himself as Christ. In the portrait shown here he is dressed in the fineries of a rich young man of fashion rather than as an humble artist-craftsman. The picture demonstrates his powers as a draughtsman, his sensitivity in the handling of colour, and the classical discipline of his compositional design.

Michelangelo Buonarroti 1475-1564

Michelangelo Buonarotti was born at Caprese, near San Sepolcro. His father was a magistrate and a member of a minor Florentine noble family. There was an element of family opposition to Michelangelo's apprenticeship as a painter in the workshop of Ghirlandaio who was at that time engaged on a fresco cycle for the church of Sta. Maria Novella in Florence. Michelangelo soon moved to a school set up by Bertoldo di Giovanni in the gardens of the Medici palace where his work quickly attracted the attention of Lorenzo de' Medici (Il Magnifico). More significantly, it was at this time that Michelangelo studied and made drawings from the works of his real 'masters', Giotto and Masaccio.

After the death of Lorenzo the political and social situation in Florence became difficult under the influence of Savonarola. In 1494 Michelangelo went to Bologna and then to Rome two years later, staying there for the following five years. In Rome his fame was established by his carving of *Bacchus* and *Pietà* in St. Peter's. The latter is his only signed work and represents the ultimate in the aims of Florentine sculptors of the 15th century.

In 1505 Michelangelo, still aged only 27, returned to Florence where he remained until 1505. During this period he produced *David,* displaying his complete understanding of human anatomy in a carving which superbly implies human energy and action. He was commissioned, together with Leonardo, to paint a large battle-piece for the Council Chamber of the Palazzo Vecchio and began work on a full size cartoon of which only a fragment known as *The Bathers* remains.

In his mid-thirties, Michelangelo was commissioned to paint the ceiling of the Sistine Chapel which he did virtually single-handed in two phases between 1508 and 1510, and 1511 and 1512. This work has ever since been regarded as one of Art's most outstanding masterpieces and has accorded to its creator the title of 'il divino'.

The last thirty years of Michelangelo's life were spent in the service of the Papacy. He began *The Last Judgement* in the Sistine Chapel in 1536 and it was

The Creation of Adam
(Sistine Chapel, Rome)

This best-known detail from the magnificent ceiling of the Sistine Chapel clearly shows, in the figure of Adam, the fullness of understanding of human anatomy attained by artists of the High Renaissance and by Michelangelo in particular. The magic of the visual conception here centres on the nearly-touching fingers of Adam and his Creator. Is the Creator gently withdrawing from a work created, or is a creative force emanating from his finger and taking human form as the spectator looks?

unveiled in 1541. The works of his old age included the *Pietà* in the Cathedral in Florence, in which the figure of Nicodemus is a self-portrait, and the *Rondanini Pietà* on which he was working at his death. In this work all his discoveries of anatomy are subordinated to abstract qualities of great emotional intensity and it has acquired a degree of respect granted to no other single piece of European sculpture.

Michelangelo was a sculptor, painter, architect and poet. Like Leonardo he admirably lived up to the Renaissance ideal of the 'universal man'.

Giorgione
c.1476/8-1510

Giorgio Barbarelli, known as Giorgione, was born in Castelfranco Veneto on the mainland north of Venice. Very little is known for certain about his life and career, but in the 1490s he probably worked in the studio of Giovanni Bellini. Still in Venice in 1506, he shared a studio with the artist Catena and, during 1506 and 1507, he worked in the Doge's Palace; unfortunately, the paintings he made there are lost.

The following year he was painting frescoes on the outside of the Fondaco dei Tedeschi, the headquarters of the German Merchants in Venice. These frescoes have also perished but they form a link with the young Titian who was working in a subordinate capacity on the decoration of the Fondaco. The contact between these two painters suggests that some of the novel ideas and developments attributed solely to Titian may have originated with Giorgione.

Giorgione neither signed nor dated his works. Although authentication of his pictures presents constant problems, it is considered certain that the famous picture *Concert Champêtre* was painted by him. The situation is further confused and complicated by his early death in 1510, aged between 32 and 34, almost certainly of the plague. He left many unfinished canvases, *Concert Champêtre* being one which was completed by pupils and associates, including Titian.

Despite the problems of uncertainty, Giorgione's work is considered by many to mark an important turning point in Venetian painting; a turning point which was to have an even longer-term effect upon the development of western European painting. He was the initiator of the 'landscape of mood' which is very well exemplified in *Tempest*. Landscape at this time in Italy was still regarded by painters as background or support to the main subject matter of a picture, and was not considered pictorially important

in itself. Giorgione made the mood of the landscape central to his purpose, subordinating detail and fully exploiting colour to that end.

Another interesting contribution to the development of western European painting was Giorgione's production of small pictures for purchase by private collectors. He was thus one of the first painters of what is now called 'easel' painting, which has now virtually displaced large mural painting.

Tempest
(Accademia, Venice)

This is an important picture in itself but it acquired another dimension of importance in the 19th century when Manet used its compositional design as the basis for his picture Le Déjeuner sur l'Herbe. *Manet's attempt so to relate 'contemporary' painting to the past, and render homage to tradition, was misunderstood; his picture was thought outrageous and was removed from exhibition in the Salon des Refusés in 1863.*

Giorgione's central subject matter is essentially the landscape and the threatening storm. The figures become an extension to the landscape, being threatened by the storm, but appear almost irrelevant or unnecessary to the picture. Colour is richly and dramatically exploited so as to heighten the picture's intensity.

Raphael   1483-1520

Raffaello Sanzio, called Raphael, one of the outstanding painters of the High Renaissance, was born in Urbino the son of a provincial painter. At an early age he came under the influence of Perugino, a prolific painter whose work is sometimes criticised for its sweetness and prettiness of colour. Raphael's *Betrothal of the Virgin* owes something to Perugino's influence but it also shows an assurance of drawing, suggesting mass and volume, never achieved by Perugino.

The two men worked together on frescoes for the Audience Chamber of the Collegio del Cambio in Perugia. Raphael rapidly outstripped Perugino and from 1504, when he went to Florence, he easily and delightedly assimilated the ideas of the great masters Michelangelo and Leonardo. The High Renaissance was created in the first decade of the 16th century and the young Raphael, only in his twenties, played an equal part in its shaping alongside Michelangelo and Leonardo.

In 1508, still only 25 years of age, Raphael was summoned to Rome by Pope Julius II and commissioned to paint frescoes in the Stanza della Segnatura, one of the rooms in the Vatican. He remained in Rome for the rest of his life and became one of the principal artists employed by the Vatican.

Besides painting frescoes in several other rooms of the Vatican he was appointed in 1514 to succeed Bramante as architect of the new St. Peter's. In 1515 and 1516 he was working on the cartoons (designs) for tapestries to be hung on the walls of the Sistine Chapel. The surviving tapestries are still in the Vatican; the cartoons are in the Victoria & Albert Museum in London, having been brought to England by King Charles I for his tapestry works at Mortlake.

In addition to this already enormous output, Raphael designed mosaics and painted portraits, notably of Popes Julius II and Leo X. He died in 1520 with his last great work for the Vatican, *The Transfiguration,* unfinished.

Raphael was always concerned to try to express in painting the relationship, as he saw it, between classical learning and Christian revelation. He remains unsurpassed in his facility of representation and in his ability to suggest the rounded form on the two dimensional surface. Some of his ideas and techniques are questioned by 20th century painters but he has had a strong impact upon the development of European art.

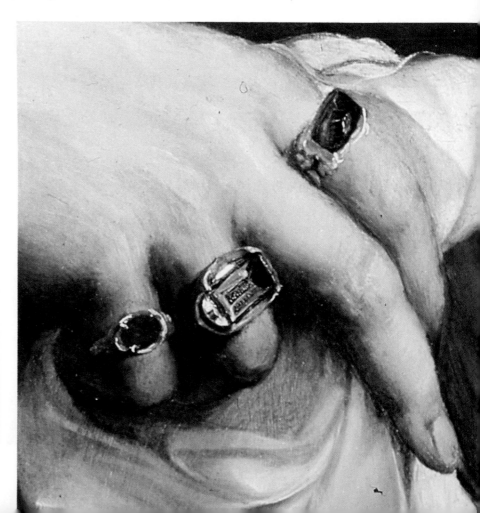

Pope Julius II
(National Gallery, London)

This fine portrait is also interesting in that it gives a clear characterisation of the man with whom Michelangelo had such disagreements. In addition it had great influence upon the painting of Cardinal Guevara by El Greco and, even more so, upon the painting of Pope Innocent X by Velázquez.

Titian   c.1490-1576

Tiziano Vecelli, or Titian, spent his early training in the studio of Giovanni Bellini. He then worked on the decoration of the Fondaco dei Tedeschi in Venice where he came under the influence of Giorgione. After Giorgione's early death Titian was to complete, with other artists, the many unfinished works of Giorgione.

Titian's own first big commission was to paint three frescoes in the Scuola del Santo in Padua. Upon the death of Bellini in 1516 he was appointed official painter to the Republic of Venice. He was gradually to throw off the influences of Bellini and Giorgione and develop his own very decided and individual style; this is well exemplified in *Venus and Cupid with Lute Player*. At about the same time, between 1516 and 1518, he produced the great *Assumption* for the Frari Church in Venice where it still hangs above the high altar. This work is dramatically vigorous; it exploits strong contrasts of light and shade and, in its suggestion of movement, indicates that Titian was moving from the strict classical control of the Renaissance into the more romantic style known as Baroque.

Titian's wife died in 1530 and for a time his work became more restrained in manner and colour. Three years later he painted the portrait of the Emperor Charles V whose personal friend he became. He was appointed court painter to the Empire and was knighted and, on the death of Charles V, he was confirmed in office by the Emperor's successor, Philip II of Spain. At the same time Titian received commissions from several of the Italian rulers, notably the Duke and Duchess of Urbino for whose son he painted *Venus of Urbino* in 1538. During the 1540s he was in Rome and Michelangelo's influence can be detected in some of the work of this time which included a remarkably frank portrait of Pope Paul III and his Farnese grandsons.

Titian lived to a great age, dying in 1576 and retaining his artistic powers and assurance to the end. He dominated Venetian painting at the height of that school's reputation. The way in which he extended the use of colour and the technique of oil painting has dominated painters ever since. His influence has been wide-ranging, constant and is ineradicable.

Venus
(National Gallery of Scotland, Edinburgh)

It is interesting to contrast this interpretation of Venus rising from the sea with that by Botticelli. In this case, the symbolic shell seems to be included merely as a gesture to tradition. Titian is more concerned to use the legend as a device for the pictorial expression of his delight in, and ability to portray, the female form and to do so with marvellously disciplined sensuousness.

Hans Holbein 1497/8-1543

Hans Holbein, the younger son of a painter of the same name, was born in Augsburg. His early training was in his father's studio but he also learned skills, craftsmanship and design from the famous goldsmiths in his town.

Renaissance ideas were now widespread and influential in northern Europe and the young Holbein was strongly affected by them. He abandoned the Gothic style inherited from his training but never abandoned the techniques he had acquired. His early portraits show that he continued his father's method of painting from very careful drawings.

In 1514 Holbein moved to Basel where he worked as a designer for book printers. One of his earliest designs was the title-page for Sir Thomas More's book *Utopia*. In 1515 he met the great philosopher and scholar Erasmus and from 1517 to 1519 he was in Lucerne from where he went into Italy and saw something of Renaissance painting at first hand. His own painting became, as a result, less harsh in colour and more monumental in composition.

After his return to Basel in 1519 he was hailed as the leading painter in that city and was commissioned to decorate the town hall with scenes of 'justice' from classical history. The work was interrupted by the unrest originating from the Reformation, and by his own journeyings abroad, and was not finished until 1530. Meanwhile, he had designed the title page for Luther's Bible in 1522 and had painted portraits of Erasmus and the Earl of Radnor in 1523. The Radnor portrait is thought to be one of Holbein's most searching character studies. In 1524 he visited France where he made further contact with Renaissance ideas and saw the work of Raphael.

The social unrest continued in Basel and there was a serious decline in patronage and so, in 1526, Holbein went to seek work in England. During this visit he produced the group portrait of the family of Sir Thomas More, of which only the initial drawing now survives. Holbein was back in Basel by 1528 only to find conditions even more difficult and so, in 1532, he returned to England where he obtained patronage from the merchants of the German Steelyards. This led to contact with the Chancellor Thomas Cromwell whose portrait he painted and through whom he obtained royal patronage. By 1536 Holbein was working for Henry VIII and he produced many versions of the portrait shown opposite.

Holbein is one of the great draughtsmen of European art but as a painter he was a sound disciple of the Italian Renaissance. He died in 1543, a victim of the plague.

Henry VIII
(Walker Gallery, Liverpool)

This version, which is described as from the 'school' of Holbein, shows the king in all his self-styled splendour as a Prince of the Renaissance. More importantly it demonstrates Holbein's assimilation of Renaissance ideas and techniques in painting. The richness of colour and texture, the understanding of light and space, and the compositional design all reflect the Renaissance influence. His own individual contribution is seen in the meticulous explanation of detail throughout the picture but particularly so in the carpet and in the drapery hanging on the right of the composition.

45

Jacopo Tintoretto
1518-1594

Jacopo Tintoretto's surname is a nickname deriving from the trade of his father who was a dyer *(un tintore).* Jacopo was born in Venice and, though little is known of his early years, it is reasonably certain that he worked for a short time in Titian's studio. By 1539 his work had acquired sufficient maturity of ideas and technique for him to establish his own studio workshop. From about 1550 the influence of Titian became more apparent in Tintoretto's work despite the great differences in their characters. But eventually Tintoretto developed a quite different personal style, attracting a quite different kind of patronage. Unscrupulous in seeking commissions, he had no hesitation in undercutting the prices of possible rivals for patronage.

Tintoretto's style evolved from many sources of inspiration. He studied and gained a great deal from the work of Michelangelo. He worked partly from wax models set in a small stage and experimented with differing sources and intensities of light played upon the scenes. This use of artificial light carries the constant preoccupation with light experienced by European artists into yet another area.

Between 1565 and 1587 Tintoretto was absorbed in the huge and splendid paintings, with their remarkable effects of trompe l'oeil (optical illusion), for the Scuola di S. Rocco in Venice. This work ranks with Michelangelo's ceiling in the Sistine Chapel in the Vatican and with Raphael's frescoes in the several rooms of the Vatican. To stand in the rooms of the Scuola di S. Rocco is a unique visual experience — one is, as it were, immersed in a vast pool of colour, light, shape and movement. This is the style and quality of work more commonly associated with Tintoretto's name though one should not undervalue the importance of the more 'easel-like' painting of *Christ walking on the*

Waters.

Most of Tintoretto's work remains in Venice and it is only there that its magnificence, and the extraordinary facility and stature of the artist, can be properly appreciated. After his death in 1594, painting in Venice suffered an eclipse for more than a century until the arrival of very different painters such as Canaletto and Tiepolo.

S. George and the Dragon
(National Gallery, London)

The feeling of movement suggested throughout the picture, particularly in the figure of the rescued damsel rushing, as it were, out of the picture, is typical of painting in the Baroque manner. The richness of colour and the confident drawing clearly demonstrate Tintoretto's pictorial powers and assurance.

Pieter Bruegel
c.1525/30-1569

Pieter Bruegel (or Breughel) the Elder was the father of a family of painters and the most significant of them. He is sometimes described as 'Peasant Bruegel' while his sons Jan and Pieter II are referred to as 'Velvet Bruegel' and 'Hell Bruegel'. The date of Pieter the Elder's birth is unknown but from the fact that he became a master painter of the Guild of Antwerp in 1551 it is assumed that he was born between 1525 and 1530.

Between 1551 and 1555 Bruegel journeyed via France to Italy, reaching as far south as Naples and Sicily. This gave him direct contact with the work of Italian artists of the Renaissance. On his return journey through the Alps he made many drawings which were remarkable for their accuracy, observational power and sensitivity.

On his return to Antwerp he designed a series of landscapes which were engraved and published. He also published a series of engravings, very much in the manner of Hieronymus Bosch and dealing with similar subjects, and his main preoccupation seems to have been with such graphic work until about 1562. In 1563 he married and moved to Brussels, from then on concentrating on painting. His paintings reflect Bosch's sense of the absurdity of mankind and the consequences of his sin and folly.

Bruegel was a considerable technician and also something of a realist; it is this that has emphasised his importance for

painters since the 19th century. The nickname 'Peasant Bruegel' should not be taken as implying that he was a peasant either in fact or in thought. He was a highly cultivated man who enjoyed the friendship of educated men and the patronage of Cardinal Granvella, the representative in the Netherlands of the Holy Roman Emperor.

Not all of Bruegel's pictures are concerned with 'genre' themes. In the last decade of his life he produced religious subjects and classical themes set in wide landscapes and these rank among his finest works. A man of great range, in both subject matter and technique, his work is the dominant feature in Flemish art between van Eyck and Rubens.

Peasant Wedding
(Kunsthistorisches Museum, Vienna)

In this lively scene Bruegel as realist and satirist is very evident. Incidental and humourous detail is acutely observed and lovingly recorded. Even the dignity of the bride, around whom the picture is stabilized, is seen with a touch of kind mockery and is overwhelmed by the bombast and absurdity of the revellers.

El Greco 1541-1614

El Greco's real name was Domenikos Theotocopoulos and he was born near Candia in Crete. Crete was at that time occupied by the Venetians and so it is quite natural that, after he had learned to paint in the Byzantine school in Crete, he went to Venice itself for further training. Little is known for certain about that period of his life but he studied and worked in Venice for some years prior to 1570 and it is thought that he worked with Titian. By 1577 he was in Toledo where he remained for the rest of his life, dying there in 1614. Despite his Cretan origins, and the early Venetian and Italian influences, he is regarded historically as a Spanish painter. The name El Greco is Spanish for 'The Greek'.

El Greco is sometimes described as a 'disciple' of Titian, though the work of Tintoretto probably made a greater impact upon him than that of Titian. He also deeply admired the work of Michelangelo and many other Italian masters. His own mature style is a uniquely personal distillation from the many widely differing experiences and influences to which he was subjected in his early life. The one thousand year cultural influence of Byzantium, which had fallen to the Turks only in 1453, was still very strong in his native island of Crete. That and the impact of the greatly different, but equally powerful, Italian Renaissance fashioned the style associated with his name.

The work of El Greco's maturity consisted mainly of religious subjects. He attempted to combine in his work the pictorial expression of profound religious emotion with supernatural vision. His picture *The Burial of Count Orgaz* is, perhaps, the most outstanding example of this attempt. At the same time he excelled in portraiture, for which he received many commissions. In addition to his painting he also worked as sculptor and architect and he designed, painted and built whole altarpieces.

Most immediately significant to the 20th century is El Greco's interest in landscape as demonstrated in the views he painted of Toledo. His highly personal and unusual use of colour, combined with broad brushwork, and his abandoning of traditional techniques, have made him of great interest to and an influence on painters of the 19th and 20th centuries.

View of Toledo
(The Metropolitan Museum of Art, New York)

This is a remarkable record of what the city looked like in relation to its landscape setting, but it is more than just a record. The dramatic mood of the picture reflects the personality of the artist as well as the climatic effects at the time of its painting. The powerful dominance of the sky in the picture's atmospheric quality, as well as in its compositional design, adds to the sense that Giorgione's influence pervades the whole picture. The colour relationships and the economy of the colour-range employed are indicative of El Greco's fundamental artistic self-discipline.

51

Caravaggio 1573-1610

Michelangelo Merisi da Caravaggio, so called after his birthplace near Milan, spent a four-year apprenticeship with a self-styled pupil of Titian and then moved to Rome, though precisely when this move took place is uncertain. In the 1590s he had gained the patronage of Cardinal del Monte for whom he produced several commissions which met with a mixed reception. He came under strong criticism for painting in the 'Venetian' manner — that is by working directly in oils on to the canvas instead of first drawing a detailed 'cartoon' from which the painting is produced.

Caravaggio's work falls into two phases. The first, falling between 1592 and 1597, was an experimental one and the work consisted of small pictures of undramatic subjects. It included a great many still lifes; this is of interest when it is recalled that the still life, as an art form in its own right, did not become firmly established until the last century. Even in his pictures such as *Supper at Emmaus* the still life objects on the table are depicted with obvious absorption and interest on the part of the artist and seem of almost equal visual importance as the four figures at the table.

The second phase, from 1597 to 1606, shows the style usually associated with Caravaggio's name. This reveals his complete mastery of pictorial story telling. Strongly contrasted light is very carefully directed and there emerges a quite new dramatic intensity to his paintings. From this use of dramatically contrasted light and shade comes the term 'Caravaggiesque'. The term is, for example, applied to some of the work of Rembrandt.

Caravaggio's development in this eight-year period was rapid and the visual experiments he made have had a far-reaching effect. He gave a new emphasis and dimension to the search for, and understanding of, the description of objects by light which had preoccupied European painters for so long.

Caravaggio was compelled to flee from Rome in 1606 after attacking a justiciary. His last four years were spent wandering between Naples, Malta and Sicily and his death, after a brawl in Naples, was reported in 1609. In fact he died of malarial fever while on his way back to Rome in 1610 in the hope of receiving a Papal Pardon.

Conversion of St. Paul
(Church of Sta. Maria del Popolo, Rome)

This picture clearly demonstrates the dramatic tension Caravaggio creates by the skilfull placing of concentrated light. The side of the horse, the upper part of the face of the man holding the horse, and the spotlighting of the fallen St. Paul all keep the eye moving and searching. The drawing is masterly, particularly in the foreshortening of the figure of St. Paul. The use of the leg of the horse and the upraised arms of St. Paul makes, in their inverted relation to each other, a novel and refreshing compositional design.

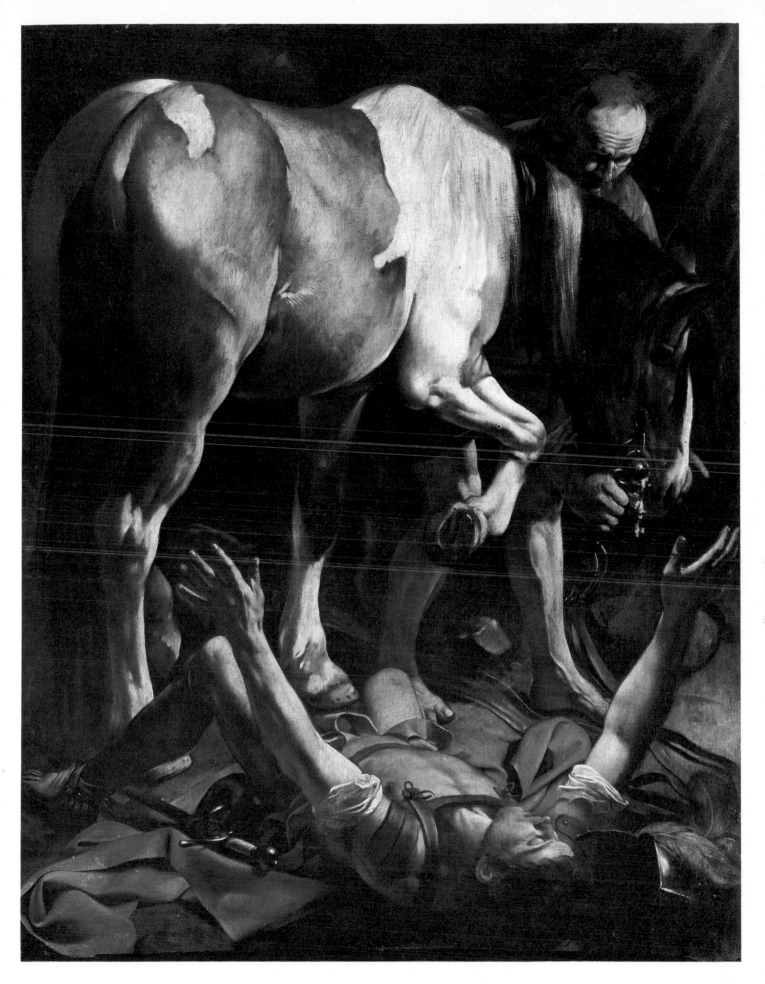

Peter Paul Rubens 1577-1640

Rubens was born in Siegen, Westphalia, the son of a protestant lawyer from Antwerp. His first teachers were three mediocre painters from Antwerp who could do little more than introduce him to Flemish artistic traditions and teach him basic techniques. He was a highly intelligent youth and gained a thorough grounding in classical scholarship with fluency in Latin and the major European languages. In 1598 he became a master painter of the Guild of St. Luke in Antwerp, and between 1600 and 1602 he was in Rome. In 1603, while on a diplomatic mission to Spain for the Duke of Mantua, he painted an equestrian portrait and made copies after Titian. The years 1605 to 1608 were spent between Genoa and Rome and from this period come portraits of Genoese patricians and an altarpiece in the church of Sta. Maria Nuova in Rome. While in Rome he studied assiduously from the antique and became familiar with the frescoes of Michelangelo and the paintings of Correggio.

By 1608 Rubens had returned to Antwerp, then the cultural capital of the Counter-Reformation in Spanish-occupied Flanders. He was appointed official painter to Archduke Albert of Austria in 1609 and in the same year married Isabella Brant. Between 1609 and 1621 he received many commissions for pictures, ceilings and altarpieces.

In 1622 he visited Paris and was commissioned to paint the series *The Life of Marie de Medici*. From this time he became a power in international diplomacy, as well as painter and designer. He charmed Philip IV of Spain and received many commissions from him. He was knighted by Charles I of England whom he assisted in the establishment of the royal art collection, while doing much of the preliminary work for the decoration of the ceiling of the Banqueting Hall of the new Whitehall Palace. Isabella Brant died in

Le Chapeau de Paille
(National Gallery, London)

The title of this picture was applied by Sir Joshua Reynolds when he saw the portrait in Antwerp in 1784. The sitter is almost certainly Susanna, sister of Rubens' second wife, Helène Fourment. It was probably a 'betrothal' portrait painted for the occasion of her second marriage to Arnold Lunden in 1622. Its outstanding artistic qualities are seen in the delicacy of colour-handling to suggest the flesh, which contrasts with the more vigorous handling and stronger colour of the clothing and the sky.

54

1626 and Rubens returned to Antwerp
in 1630 and married the 16-year-old
Helène Fourment.

It has been said of Rubens that he was
a highly successful businessman who ran
a large factory, employing an army of
specialist assistants. In his defence it
must be said that he operated in the
direct tradition of the studio/workshop
which had existed throughout the
Renaissance, and it must be emphasized
that the original compositional designs
were always his and that no work left
Rubens' studio without his personal
scrutiny and final approval.

Rubens himself worked with great
speed and his output was very large. His
draughtsmanship shows great authority
and all his paintings have a wonderful
luminosity of colour. He died in 1640,
leaving a great reputation which
suffered eclipse in the 19th century, but
now his work seems to be enjoying a re-
appraisal.

Frans Hals   1580/5-1666

Frans Hals was the only important member of a whole family of painters which included his brothers Dirk and Joost, and five of his sons: Jan, Harmen, Claes, Frans II and Reynier. Hals was probably born in Antwerp between 1580 and 1585, of Flemish parents, who settled in Holland and finally in Haarlem where he spent the rest of his long life.

Hals' first significant work, painted c.1616, was *The Banquet of the Officers of the St. George Militia Company*. There was no precedent for the vigorous characterisation of the individuals in this remarkable group portrait, nor evidence of any other artist's influence. It also reveals his virtuosity as a colourist.

It was in the 1620s that he painted the famous *The Laughing Cavalier* which demonstrates his knowledge of the caravaggiesque, probably gained from the links he had at this time with painters of the Utrecht School. Although the first part of his career had been devoted mainly to 'genre' paintings, he now became, at the height of his popularity, primarily a portraitist.

During this period he produced no less than five large group paintings of Civic Guards, each of which presented enormous problems of compositional design. The problem was caused because all of the commissioners expected to see themselves equally depicted as they were each paying a share of the price. Gradually his pictures became simpler in composition; a more chromatic colour scheme replaced the earlier bright colour, and very few painters matched his technical facility and certainty of touch.

For nearly three centuries Hals' work was virtually unknown and ignored, and from his long life there remain only about two hundred authenticated paintings and no drawings. It is possible, even probable, that he worked directly in paint, without any preliminary drawing, a method now quite common but most unusual before the 19th century. His full worth and importance was only recognised by the Realist and Impressionist painters, and the informality of his group portraits were of particular interest to Manet.

Hals had a difficult life which was constantly plagued by financial difficulties; even at the height of his fame he was being sued by tradesmen for unpaid bills. In his last years he was destitute and the municipal authorities of Haarlem awarded him a small stipend during the four years before his death in 1666. Some of his work may be seen in the Rijksmuseum in Amsterdam, but the fullness of his range can only be appreciated in the Frans Hals Museum in Haarlem.

The Laughing Cavalier
(Wallace Collection, London)

For many people this is the only known picture by Frans Hals. It is a masterpiece of portraiture with the simplicity of the background concentrating attention upon the figure. The colour is rich and fully descriptive of texture, yet it is also restrained and disciplined. The drawing is superbly stated in the three-quarter stance of the body, the cast of the head and the slightly downward look from the eyes.

57

Anthony van Dyck
1599-1641

Van Dyck was born the son of a silk merchant, and although Flemish by birth he is regarded as an English painter. Even as a youth the excellence of his technique and the maturity of his style were exceptional. He began an apprenticeship at the age of 11 and by the age of 16 he was using assistants and selling his work. This was highly irregular as he was not yet enrolled as a Master Painter of the Guild of St. Luke. He did enrol as such in 1618 and, still in his teens, he entered the workshop of Rubens. Van Dyck's experience there

had a decided and lasting influence upon his subsequent development.

Van Dyck first visited England in 1620 and King James I was anxious to appoint him Court Painter, but Van Dyck declined. He stayed only a few months and in 1621 started four years of journeying in Italy — Rome, Venice, Genoa, Florence and Palermo. In Rome he felt outshone by artists such as Domenichino, Guercino and Bernini. In Genoa he received and executed many portrait commissions and it was in Genoa, perhaps, that Van Dyck evolved the elegance of style associated with his name. His Flemish vigour was gradually replaced by a more subtle use of colour.

Between 1626 and 1632 he spent much of his time in Antwerp and this is the period of some of his finest portraits. He showed greater sensitivity to the individuality of the sitters than had many painters, including Rubens. The religious paintings of this period suggest the influence of Titian, Rubens and Correggio.

From 1632 until his death in 1641, Van Dyck was in England; it was a prolific period. He had immense prestige at court and was knighted by King Charles I. His work was in great demand and he established the pattern for the tradition of portrait painting in England which lasted for at least another century and a half. Particularly famous among the portraits of this period are the equestrian portraits of Charles I and the triple portrait of the king which was sent to Bernini to serve as a model for a bust.

A little known area of activity in which Van Dyck indulged was the painting of landscapes in water colour. This is an unexpected fore-shadowing of a section of art in which the painters of his adopted country later made an exceptional contribution to the development of European painting.

Charles I of England
(Louvre, Paris)

Light and shade do not have the dramatic intensity of contrast which is seen in the work of Caravaggio. They are disposed in more subtle ways yet are obviously fully understood and cleverly exploited. The off-centre placing of the King counterbalanced by the shadowy figures of the attendants, the reflected light on the horse's mane, and the leaning tree trunk give the picture a compositional design which is at once spontaneous and yet formal. This formality intentionally underlines the regality of the main subject matter. The handling of colour is masterly and the mood of the picture owes something to the influence of Giorgione.

Diego Velázquez 1599-1660

Diego Velázquez was born in Seville, of Portuguese origin, and lived there until the age of 14. Between 1610 and 1616 he was apprenticed to Francisco Pacheco whose daughter he later married. From Pacheco he received assistance in the acquisition of a sound technique and some knowledge of the works of Renaissance painters from both Italy and northern Europe. But already, at the age of 18, Velázquez was artistically ahead of his master.

His work at this time consisted mainly of everyday subjects with still life objects and sometimes a religious scene in the background. Painted in a naturalistic, non-idealistic way, they had strong chiaroscuro (light and shade, from the Italian 'chiara' meaning light or clear and 'oscuro' meaning dark or shade) and show some influence from the work of Caravaggio.

In 1622 Velázquez paid a short visit to Madrid and returned there permanently the following year to become Court Painter to Philip IV. His first aim was to break down the stiff and formal style of Spanish court portraiture. In 1629 he paid his first visit to Italy where he studied the work of contemporary

painters in Rome and also that of the masters of the Renaissance. A second visit to Italy between 1649 and 1651 was mainly concerned with the purchasing of antiques and paintings for the Spanish royal collection. These direct contacts with Italy had a profound influence upon his own work and his portrait of *Pope Innocent X* is very much in the line of Raphael's *Pope Julius II* and Titian's *Pope Paul III. The Rokeby Venus,* the only nude painted by Velázquez, owes something to the influences of Titian and Giorgione though it is less sensual and more realist than nudes by either artist.

The picture *Las Meninas* (Spanish for 'Maids of Honour') is a mixture, unusual for Velázquez, of portraiture and allegory. The central figure is the Infanta, or Princess, Margareta Teresa but the explanation for the inclusion of other figures, including himself, and other elements has been debated ever since it was painted. The picture so impressed Picasso that, in 1957, he used it as the theme for a series of forty-four variations.

Surrender of Breda, depicting an incident in the Dutch wars of Independence and painted by Velázquez in 1634, was one of a series of battle-pieces painted for the Hall of the Realms in the royal palace of Buen Retiro. In 1659 Velázquez was invested as a Knight of the Order of Santiago. He died in August 1660 and is buried in the church of San Juan Bautista in Madrid. His wife survived him by only eight days and is buried by his side.

Surrender of Breda
(Prado, Madrid)

This picture makes an important contribution to the painting of contemporary historical subjects. It is convincing in its realism and yet the central shape, in which the one figure hands the key to the other, is so emphasized in colour and tone as to make it an almost abstract shape. This is compositional design at its most subtle and best. The visually effective use of pikes and spears recalls Uccello's Battle of San Romano.

Claude Lorraine 1600-1682

Claude Gellée, called Lorraine, was born near Nancy in France. At about the age of 12 he entered the household of the Roman painter, Agostino Tassi, as a pastrycook. By 1619 he was working as a painter's assistant in Tassi's studio and there is specific record of him working with Tassi on the decoration of a villa at about this time. In his early twenties he spent two years in Naples where the coastline so delighted him that he made many drawings which he used in subsequent pictures. In 1625 he was back in Lorraine and, through collaboration with another painter, developed the interest in classical architecture which is frequently used in his pictures, such as *The Embarkation of the Queen of Sheba*.

In 1627 Claude returned to Rome, where he stayed until his death in 1682. By the end of the 1630s he had acquired a considerable reputation as a landscape painter and his work was in such demand that he made copies of his pictures to guard against forgeries. The collection of these copies is known as the 'Liber Veritatis' and this idea was borrowed nearly two centuries later by Turner, one of Claude's greatest admirers.

The years 1640 to 1660 were Claude's real maturing period. He had taken up the European artists' preoccupation with light and had developed great sensitivity

to the tonal values of light and to atmospheric effects. Indeed, the real theme of his pictures became the mood of landscape as represented by light and colour. All his efforts were directed to the elaboration of a personal style which would effectively depict this visual experience. He actually brought the sun, the source of light, into the picture. He drew up strict colour and compositional formulae, which he applied to all his pictures, by which the foreground, middle and far distances all have precise colour, light and tonal values.

Claude greatly loved the countryside around Rome and made many sketches in bistre and wash which are remarkable for their breadth of technique; they are of great interest to 20th-century artists. Bistre is a brown pigment prepared by boiling soot; it produces a rich warm brown somewhat darker than sepia. His work was of great interest to Turner in particular and to the French Impressionists in general. He played an important part in the evolution of the philosophy that light is the real subject matter for the painter.

The Embarkation of the Queen of Sheba
(National Gallery, London)

This is an example which includes nearly all of the methods employed by Claude to give pictorial expression to his theories and discoveries. The architectural features, with their classical references, are used as an inner frame to concentrate attention upon the horizon which is the main focal point of the composition. Colour and spatial recession are both made to serve the main preoccupation with light.

Rembrandt van Rijn   1606-1669

Rembrandt van Rijn was born in Leyden, the son of a miller. He enrolled as a student at the University of Leyden in 1620 but left after a few months to study painting. He worked for three years with a minor painter called Swanenburgh but this was followed by a more valuable six months in the studio of Pieter Lastman of Amsterdam where he was introduced to the work of Caravaggio and Elsheimer which had a lasting influence upon him.

In 1625 Rembrandt set himself up as an artist in Leyden. Most of his pictures at this time were on historical themes but he also began to work on the famous series of self portraits. He was already making effective use of 'chiaroscuro' and exploiting the full potential of oil painting, including the use of impasto (the thickness of pigment as opposed to its colour).

Rembrandt moved to Amsterdam about six years later and his reputation was immediately made with his picture *Anatomy Lesson of Dr. Tulp.* For the following decade he was the city's leading portraitist. His marriage to Saskia van Uylenborch in 1634 and the dowry and good social connections she brought with her all contributed to his establishment as an artist. A son, Titus, was born to them in 1641 but Saskia died in the following year, the year in which

The Night Watch
(Rijksmuseum, Amsterdam)

This title was applied to the picture in 1800 when it was so overlaid with varnish that it looked like a night scene. Its proper title is The Corporalship of Captain Banning Cocq's Civic Guard *and it is now cleaned. As an example of group portraiture it is a masterpiece with subtle emphasis placed on light and shade.*

---

he painted the famous picture known as *The Night Watch* which is reproduced opposite and below.

It is from this time that a change of direction and a new emphasis begins to show in Rembrandt's work. From conventional portraiture he makes a greater attempt to give visual expression to the inner life and character of his sitters. His self portraits, important in themselves as works of art, played a decisive part in this disciplined effort. At the same time, he began to make studies direct from nature in which 'mood' dominates, an indication of his awareness of the work and ideas of Giorgione. At this time, too, he produced much graphic work, particularly etchings.

As he began to paint more for himself, rather than to the dictates of patronage, commissions declined and he was declared bankrupt in 1656. His works, belongings and collection of paintings by other artists were auctioned in 1657 in an effort to clear his debts.

Rembrandt's output was prodigious and in the last year of his life he produced two works of exceptional quality: *The Jewish Bride* and *The Return of the Prodigal Son*. At his death in 1669 his work was known throughout Europe and he is now generally considered to be the greatest painter of the Dutch 17th-century school. His etchings have always retained their appeal and his work and ideas have exerted a strong influence upon all painters since his time.

Pieter de Hoogh 1629-1684?

Pieter de Hoogh, although born in Rotterdam and dying in Amsterdam, is usually referred to as one of the Delft school of painters. He must, therefore, have known his contemporary Vermeer and have been influenced by him. There are obvious similarities in the subject matter adopted by both artists; the interiors of houses with figures absorbed in their usual daily activities. The mood of the pictures is tranquil and peaceful and there is some suggestion of influence from the work of Caravaggio in the manner in which light is used. An indication of the source of light, a window, is usually implied and the window is sometimes incorporated into the composition.

The portrayal of detail, whether of furnishing, clothing or objects about the room, is sensitive and acute. This approach to, and use of, subject matter is usually referred to as 'genre' painting. There is no direct equivalent for this word in English but it is used to describe the depiction of scenes from everyday life. Most of the Dutch painters of the 17th century, with the exception of 'marine' artists, worked in this field to a greater or lesser extent.

In de Hoogh's work the interior of a building is treated with exactly the same importance as the people within or the activities in which the people are engaged. The whole is conceived as a unity and it is interesting to recall that, two centuries before, Piero Della Francesca's pictures were also conceived as a unity of figures in their setting. In short, de Hoogh gave a new and personal emphasis to an already established visual principle. His work is at its best when depicting a sunny yard with the interior of a house beyond or when, as in the case of *An Interior Scene,* he shows light pouring into the interior of a rich merchant's house.

In 1667 de Hoogh settled in Amsterdam and from then on the quality of his work sadly deteriorated. It became less simple, direct and realist and altogether less convincing. The pictures depicted rather false scenes of life in high society and quantity of output tended to replace quality.

An Interior Scene
(National Gallery, London)

This picture is very typical of the best of de Hoogh's work. The window as the source of light is included in the composition and the way in which objects are described by light is clearly understood and stated. Linear perspective is employed without being too obvious or dominant and the colour is rich and lively. The figure of the woman standing before the fireplace would appear to be a late addition, to correct an imbalance in the compositional design, for the painting of the receding tiles of the floor can be seen through the bottom of her skirt.

Johannes Vermeer   1632-1675

Jan Vermeer was born and died in Delft. He was the son of a silk merchant who was also something of an art dealer and a tavern keeper.

In 1653 Vermeer married and entered the local painters' guild. On the death of his father two years later he took over the family business from which he endeavoured to provide for his family which eventually included eleven children. He was always in debt, yet there is no evidence of him ever selling his paintings in his lifetime. Apart from that, remarkably little is known about the man and his life.

The bulk of Vermeer's work is 'genre' in style. The pictures almost invariably show a room with light coming in from the left. The window, the source of the light, is often included in the composition and there is usually one solitary figure in the room, the model being his wife. The predominant colours he used are yellow, blue and grey.

Vermeer's compositions have an abstract simplicity which imbues them with a grandness of conception totally surpassing their actual small size. This is one of the reasons why his work has proved of such interest to artists in this century. He did produce two outstanding pictures on a larger scale; *The View of Delft* and *Artist in his Studio*. The former is the only landscape view he is known to have produced yet it has the appearance of much experience and great mastery in this area of artistic activity.

Sadly, there are only thirty-six authenticated pictures by Vermeer in existence today. It could be assumed that he worked very slowly; that he painted only in his spare time; or that the great explosion in Delft in 1654 destroyed his early works. Whatever the explanation, his output remains small, averaging only three per year. What matters more is the technical facility and artistic sensitivity apparent in all the works which do exist and how this was achieved. He must have been conversant with the work of his contemporaries such as Rembrandt and with wider influences from European art.

Vermeer's work fell into total eclipse after his death and was virtually unknown until van Gogh wrote enthusiastically about it in 1879.

Artist in his Studio
(*Kunsthistorisches Museum, Vienna*)

Vermeer creates the sensation of looking through a subsidiary frame into an intimate interior. This subsidiary frame is made up of the rich drapery in the foreground, the beams of the ceiling, and the dark line down the side of the map hanging on the wall. The light comes from a window which is implied rather than stated. The rich drapery, the chandelier, the musical instrument and the map all indicate a man of culture and education.

Antoine Watteau 1684-1721

Antoine Watteau was born in Valenciennes and went to Paris in 1702. From 1703 to 1708 he worked with Gillot, a painter of theatrical scenery, which stimulated his interest in the theatre, costume and scenes from daily life. In 1708 when he joined Claude Audran, Keeper of the Luxembourg Palace, he gained access to the series of paintings by Rubens — *The Life of Marie de Medici*. He greatly admired the work of Rubens and came to know at

---

'La Gamme d'Amour'
(National Gallery, London)

This is perhaps the most widely known of Watteau's paintings. It is certainly a clear example of the type of picture known as 'fête-champêtres'. The basis of the composition is a diagonal cross with the musical instrument at the centre of the diagonals. The mood of the picture is peaceful and relaxed, a quality supported by the restraint of colour and texture. The delicacy of treatment of plant growth demonstrates the eye for detail typical of the genre painter. The dimly lit face of the carved bust on the plinth above the head of the musician seems to be viewing the idyllic scene with gentle cynicism.

first hand the works of Flemish and Italian masters, including those of the Venetian school.

Watteau was known as 'le peintre Flamand', Valenciennes having been until recently part of Flanders, so it is fitting that he should emulate the work of Rubens, one of the greatest of Flemish painters. In 1717 Watteau submitted his diploma picture entitled *Embarkation for the Island of Cythera* and this is possibly his finest work. Suffering from tuberculosis, he went to consult Queen Anne's physician in London in 1719. The winter spent in England did not improve his health and he died in Paris aged only 37.

Watteau was an unusual mixture of two artists in one. The first was a straightforward genre painter with a searching eye for the pictorial possibilities of ordinary events in everyday life. The second was the highly sensitive and sophisticated designer of fêtes-champêtres, depicting scenes of restrained dalliance in gentle parkland, in which his exquisitely dressed figures are immobilised in their enjoyment of the moment, like insects fossilised in amber. His importance was in freeing French painting from the overbearing academic influence of Italian painting. He began the creation of a Parisian style, setting the tone for 18th-century French painters such as Boucher and Fragonard until the Revolution and the emergence of Jacques Louis David and Neo-Classicism.

As a colourist Watteau was an undoubted master but he was careless in technique and many of his paintings are in bad condition. He is said to be the first painter to use 'divisionism'. This method uses the surface of the picture as the palette; for example, strokes of blue and yellow are placed on the canvas to give an effect of green instead of using a green which has been pre-mixed on a palette. This technique is thought to give greater vitality to the picture and was adopted and extended by the Impressionists and Post-Impressionists. Together with Chardin, Watteau was the most important pre-Revolution painter in 18th-century France.

William Hogarth   1697-1764

William Hogarth was apprenticed at the age of 15 to an engraver of silver plate, where he learned to work in the rococo tradition. The word 'rococo' derives from the French 'rocaille', a shell, and is generally used to describe art forms which are highly ornamental. The style was most popular around 1700 in the France of Louis XIV.

In 1720 Hogarth was established in London as a copper engraver of bill-heads and book illustrations. He attended part-time drawing classes at the St. Martin's Lane Academy where he did not progress very well. Later he assisted in the foundation of a drawing academy which was the forerunner of the Royal Academy Schools. He then studied under Sir James Thornhill, whose daughter he married in 1728, and in the following years he began to make an impression with small 'conversation-piece' paintings.

In 1730 he set himself up as a portrait painter and simultaneously began the 'sequences of anecdotal pictures pointing a moral and satirizing social abuses' by which he is best known. These include *The Harlot's Progress*, painted in 1731 and later destroyed by fire; *The Rake's Progress*, painted in 1735 and now in the Sir John Soane Museum, London; and *Marriage à la Mode*, probably the most widely known and reproduced, painted between 1742 and 1744 and now in the National Gallery,

London. There were other 'sequences' and all were painted with a view to them being engraved. The engravings sold widely and were very popular with all classes of people. They were much pirated, too, and this led to the enactment of the Copyright Act of 1735, designed to protect artists from copyists.

Hogarth was equally proficient as a painter and as an engraver and, in his own self-estimation, he 'possessed a good eye, a fondness for drawing and a taste for mimicry'. He also saw himself as the defender of English common sense against continental fashions and mannerisms. He tilted equally at pedantry, affectation and immorality. His book *The Analysis of Beauty,* published in 1753, insists that the views of the practising artist should receive greater consideration than those of the collector or critic.

By the time he died in 1764 Hogarth had made a significant contribution to painting and to the position of the artist in England.

The Election
(The Soane Museum, London)

One in a sequence of four pictures bearing the same title, this is subtitled 'canvassing for votes'. The central foreground consists of a voter being canvassed by representatives of both sides in an election. The poster inscribed 'Punch Candidate for Guzzledown', and the lion holding a fleur-de-lys may be oblique references to contemporary governmental incompetence and the poor condition of British fortunes at sea. Outside 'The Crown' in the middle distance a riot has broken out, but behind the turmoil lies the imperturbably English countryside. Hogarth fully demonstrates his powers as draughtsman, colourist, satirist and social commentator.

Giovanni Antonio Canaletto 1697-1768

Antonio Canal (Canaletto) was born of a family of painters in 1697. His earliest work must have been scenery painting with his father and brother in the theatres of Venice. In his own words he 'repudiated the theatre' in 1719, went to Rome and turned his attention to 'vedute' (views) of landscape and topographical subjects.

Returning to Venice in 1723, he collaborated in producing decorative canvasses for the Duke of Richmond. These were 'vedute capriccii', or dramatic and imaginary picturesque views of Venice with strong contrasts of light and shade. He rapidly established his reputation, his work having the smooth and precise handling of both drawing and colour which remained his characteristic throughout the rest of his career.

By the 1740s, Canaletto's patrons were chiefly English collectors, notably the Dukes of Richmond and Bedford and Joseph Smith, British Consul in Venice at the time. As a natural result of such patronage he went to England in 1746 where he received many commissions for views of London and for paintings of the country mansions of the landed gentry. However, this patronage declined after a time and, in his disillusionment, his work became stilted and lifeless. By 1755 he had returned to Venice.

Apart from the topographical paintings so much associated with his name, Canaletto also produced many pen and wash drawings and some very remarkable graphic work, especially in the form of etchings. After his return to Venice he produced a set of twelve elaborate drawings of ceremonies in which the Doge of Venice participated. These are known from engravings from which Guardi later made paintings. Canaletto was elected a member of the Venetian Academia in 1765 only three years before his death in 1768.

The British Consul, Joseph Smith, eventually sold his library and paintings, including many Canalettos, to King George III of England. This fact, plus the work Canaletto did during the years he was living and working in England, has resulted in that country having the largest concentration of Canalettos. Their ready availability played an influential part in the development of English watercolour painting and, in turn, upon the development of landscape painting in France throughout the 19th century.

Eton College
(National Gallery, London)

This picture shows the extent of Canaletto's sympathetic assimilation of the English landscape. It shows, too, a sensitive response to the expectations of English patronage. Colour, drawing and light effects are highly typical of Canaletto's mature style. Compositionally, the dark tree and bank on the left and the two trees on the right hold, in a broken circle, the inner incidents with their clever intervals of the taller buildings.

Francesco Guardi 1712-1793

Francesco Guardi was one of a family of painters with a studio workshop in Venice. Giacomo Guardi, the father, started the workshop which was continued by his sons Gian-Antonio, one of the founders of the Academy in Venice, and Francesco who is now the most famous and considered to be the best artist of the family. The two brothers sometimes worked together on the same picture.

From the middle of the 18th century, Francesco began to specialise in 'vedute', or topographical scenes, very much in the style of his popular fellow Venetian, Canaletto. In addition to the straight 'veduta' (the word means 'scene' in Italian) there is the 'veduta ideata', which is a purely imaginary view made up from the artist's memory and imagination, and the 'veduta capriccio' which places architecturally correct buildings in fantastic and unlikely relationships. Piranesi, Canaletto and Guardi are the best-known exponents of this pictorial art form, but it is probably the invention of northern artists such as

Paul and Mattheus Bril who were working in Italy in the 16th century.

Francesco worked in all the 'veduta' variations but his work was not so popular as that of Canaletto and he received only half the prices paid to the latter. Francesco's work does not possess the same meticulous precision and exactness of delineation as that of Canaletto. Guardi was much more excited by the vibrant reflective relationships between water and buildings. His pictures, which are generally rather small in size, have a spontaneity and freshness which show his quick and perceptive reaction to visual experience. His style and especially his drawing is, on close investigation, unmistakeable and easily distinguishable from that of Canaletto.

To the taste of his own day Guardi's work appeared rough and unfinished. That has not prevented the repeated copying of his work ever since his death in 1793. His work has made a greater appeal to more recent taste and is now highly respected.

The Doge's Palace
(National Gallery, London)

This picture has remarkable affinities with The Feast of the Ascension in Venice *by Canaletto. The basin in front of the Doge's Palace is viewed from almost exactly the same point. In the Guardi version the foreground is less busy with detail and incident. The prow and furled sail of the boat on the left greatly assist the spectator in his appreciation of the unity of colour in the picture and the reflection of water and sky.*

George Stubbs 1724-1806

George Stubbs was born in Liverpool, the son of a currier — a dresser and colourer of leather after its tanning. Stubbs was virtually self-taught and received no regular training either as draughtsman or painter. At the age of 16 he met Hamlet Winstanley, an engraver employed in copying the paintings by old masters in Lord Derby's gallery at Knowsley Hall, and through this relationship he had his first experience of the great tradition of European painting. For a time he worked as a portrait painter in Leeds, at the same time studying human and animal anatomy in York. After journeying in Italy and Morocco, an experience which extended his knowledge of European art, he settled in London in 1759.

In 1766 Stubbs published his *Anatomy of the Horse* upon which he had spent ten years of preparation, including eighteen months drawing from dissected horses. He himself engraved all the plates for the illustration of the book and it quickly gained him an international reputation. His reputation for accuracy and beauty still holds among animal painters, animal lovers and veterinary surgeons.

The book's success established for Stubbs a successful career as a painter of horses. He was regularly commissioned for portraits of horses; sometimes by themselves and other times accompanied by their grooms and owners. In 1780 Stubbs was elected an Associate of the Royal Academy but, because of a dispute with the Academy, he never became a full Academician.

From 1795 until his death in 1806 he worked on drawings for *The Comparative Anatomy of Man, the Tiger and the Fowl* which, like its forerunner, is thorough and accurate in detailed information and beautiful in its draughtsmanship. The text and 125 drawings for this intended publication

Gimcrack with a Groom on Newmarket Heath (detail)
(Private Collection)

Although Stubbs is normally associated with the painting of horses, this detail shows that he was equally adept at painting the human form. His treatment of the groom's facial features underlines that he was a master at observing anatomical detail and human expression.

were found in 1957 in the Public Library in Worcester, Mass., USA.

Stubbs' paintings show a genuine feeling for form and for spatial relationships and their organisation. Much of his work is 'genre' in content but a romantic streak breaks through occasionally as in *Horse frightened by a Lion,* a picture which might be said to foreshadow some of the work of Delacroix and Géricault. He was much more than an accomplished painter of horseflesh. He was a gifted artist of great technical facility and liveliness of imagination.

Thomas Gainsborough 1727-1788

Thomas Gainsborough was born in Sudbury, Suffolk in England. By 1740 he was in London where he worked for the next few years under the French engraver, Gravelot. He returned to Sudbury in 1746 and, in 1756, he set himself up as a portrait painter in the neighbouring port of Ipswich. His work at this time consisted mainly of portrait heads though he also painted some half-length portraits and one or two group portraits. The picture *Heneage Lloyd and his Sister* is one such and belongs to this period. His patrons were the town merchants of Ipswich and the local country squires. This early work shows influences from French engraving and Dutch landscape painting.

In 1760 Gainsborough moved to Bath where his patrons were members of Society. The free and elegant style associated with his name began to develop at this time and is seen best in the full-length portraits. *Blue Boy* exemplifies this clearly and also reveals Van Dyck's influence upon this phase of Gainsborough's development.

In 1768 Gainsborough was elected a founder member of the Royal Academy. After making London his permanent headquarters in 1774 he became the favourite painter of the Royal family, painting several portraits of them. He was, though, never appointed court painter and, to his great chagrin, he was not even given a knighthood like his rival, Joshua Reynolds. The appointment of the latter as first President of the Royal Academy was also a bitter pill to swallow.

Although best known as a portrait painter, Gainsborough preferred to paint landscape. He regarded the former as his profession and the latter as his pleasure. He continued to paint landscapes long after leaving the country for the city. He frequently made landscape compositions from memory and imagination, using studio arrangements of grasses, leaves and flowers. His arch-rival Reynolds referred to the style Gainsborough evolved for the painting of foliage as 'fried parsley'. There was little love lost between the two, and rivalry between them ended only with Gainsborough's death in 1788.

Gainsborough was an uncomplicated artist/craftsman, being no theorist or intellectual, but his remarkable individuality and sheer delight in painting shine through everything he produced.

Mrs. Siddons
(National Gallery, London)

This portrait of the great actress demonstrates Gainsborough's powers as a portraitist through the clear, firm and expressive delineation of her features and the expert painterly handling of pigment to suggest the widely varying textures of flesh, hair, material and fur.

Jean-Honoré Fragonard 1732-1806

Jean-Honoré Fragonard was born in Grasse in France and his name and works are inextricably linked with the frivolity of the reigns of the French Kings Louis XV and Louis XVI. This is the more surprising since he was, for a short time, the pupil of Chardin whose work is so different in both style and content.

In 1752 Fragonard won the Prix de Rome and worked in the French Academy in Rome between 1756 and 1761. While there he showed more interest in the work of the living artist Tiepolo than in the work of the old masters. He also travelled in southern Italy and Sicily and developed the beginnings of his landscape style as a result of his experiences there. He returned to Paris in 1761 and was elected a member of the Academy in 1766, the year in which he painted *The Swing* which is so typical of his work.

Fragonard married in 1769 and his work for the next few years was almost entirely concerned with family scenes and children. He was patronised by the famous and influential royal mistresses, Madame de Pompadour and Madame du Barry. In 1773 he toured through Italy, Germany and Holland, and was greatly impressed with the work of Rembrandt and other Dutch painters.

The French Revolution ruined Fragonard. His patrons were the main subjects of attack from the revolutionaries and the style of his work, and the society it depicted, was anathema to the new regime. Jacques Louis David, virtual dictator of the arts under the Revolution, showed some sympathy and gave what material help he could. Fragonard attempted to adapt himself and his ideas to the Neo-Classical approach as expounded by David, but failed and died in poverty in 1806.

Fragonard was largely the victim of his times. He was not without respect for the traditions from the past and he was influenced in technique and colour by Frans Hals, Ruisdael and Rubens. He was a painter of great versatility and was able to use many styles and techniques. If he had a weakness it was that he did not pursue any one line with sufficient singleness of purpose or in sufficient depth. This gave his work an appearance of superficiality which hid its more serious intrinsic artistic quality. All his works express his own personal verve, vitality and spontaneity.

The Swing
(Wallace Collection, London)

Baron St. Julien who commissioned this picture said: "I desire that you should paint Madame (his mistress) on a swing which is being set in motion by a bishop. You must place me where I can have a good view of the legs of the pretty little thing". The lady on the swing is appropriately positioned at the centre of two crossing diagonals. The colour is handled with confidence and ease and is delightfully appropriate to the light-heartedness of the subject matter.

Francisco de Goya 1746-1828

Francisco Goya was born in Saragossa in 1746, the son of a master gilder. He first studied in Saragossa until his unruly behaviour made it advisable for him to leave the city for a time. He went to Madrid and worked for a court painter, Francisco Bayeu, whose sister he married in 1773. During this period he had made a brief visit to Rome.

Between 1776 and 1791 Goya painted a series of cartoons for the royal tapestry factory, their subject matter ranging from the idyllic to everyday realistic scenes. His fame and reputation spread widely. He was elected to the Academy of San Fernando in 1780; appointed its assistant director of painting in 1785; and in 1789 he was nominated as a court painter to King Charles IV.

His early portraits were stiff but the influence of Velázquez vitalized and brought a more natural quality to his work. Between 1792 and 1794 Goya suffered a strange illness and became deaf, an affliction which made him much more introverted. Appointed director of painting at the San Fernando Academy in 1795, his greatest portraits were produced during this period.

At about this time Goya began to work as an etcher, technically influenced by Rembrandt, on themes depicting highly imaginative scenes in which a nightmareish quality and menace over-shadow the humour. Other themes attacked abuses in the church and current social attitudes. In 1799 he produced a set of eighty-two etchings entitled *Los Caprichos* giving savage and satirical pictorial expression to his views at that time.

In 1799 he was appointed Chief Court Painter and in 1800 painted the group portrait *The Family of Charles IV*. This seems quite cruel in its frank depiction of physical absurdities but no apparent satire was intended. The two versions of the *Maja*, clothed and nude, also belong

to this period.

Under the rule of Joseph Bonaparte he retained his position as Chief Court Painter but his duties decreased. His picture *3 May 1808* and his sixty-five etchings entitled *Los Desastros de la Guerra* (The Disasters of War) express his reaction to the French occupation. They form a strong pictorial protest against the savagery and horror of war and are only equalled by Picasso's *Guernica*.

Goya still retained his position when the Bourbons were restored in 1814 but his responsibilities lessened. In 1819 he was seriously ill for a second time and between 1820 and 1822 he painted fourteen large murals known as the 'Black' paintings; painted almost entirely in blacks, browns and greys, they express his morbid outlook at the time.

In 1824 Goya left Spain and settled in Bordeaux. Here he experimented in the new medium of lithography and his paintings of the period foreshadow, in their breadth and technique, the work of the Impressionists. He was a prolific and versatile artist and his work expressed a great range of emotion as well as technical mastery. He claimed to have had three masters: Nature, Velázquez and Rembrandt.

---

3 May 1808
(Prado, Madrid)

An extraordinary picture where visual directness and honesty make no effort to spare the spectator's feelings. Attention is focused upon the defiant, but hopeless, group of victims by the effect of spotlighting. The impersonality of the shooting squad, the intense emotion of the victims, the sparseness of the hillside, and the permanence of the buildings in the background, all reinforce the central theme.

Jacques Louis David 1748-1825

Jacques Louis David was distantly related to the painter Boucher at whose instigation he was sent to study under Vien in Paris in 1765. He won the Prix de Rome and was at the French Academy in Rome between 1775 and 1781. This was an important and formative period for him and he greatly enjoyed his studies of the classical and the antique. He became strongly attracted to the theories of Neo-Classicism as expounded by the artist Mengs, who believed that visual perfection would be best expressed by combining the Greek tradition of design with the expressiveness of Raphael, the chiaroscuro of Correggio and the colour of Titian.

On his return to France, David was elected to the Academy and during the next decade he established his pictorial reaction to, and rejection of, the frivolity of rococo are. He became the effective leader of Neo-Classicism and paintings such as *The Oath of the Horatii* and *Death of Socrates* spread the influence of Neo-Classicism well beyond the boundaries of France.

After the outbreak of the Revolution he became a Deputy, voted for the execution of the King, and was unchallenged as the 'Painter of the Revolution'. His role in the arts was dictatorial; he replaced the Academy with a new Institut des Arts, and staged huge 'Festivals of Reason' in the streets of Paris.

The picture *Death of Marat* is one of three 'martyrs' of the Revolution that he painted and, interestingly, the quite different painting of *Madame Recamier* also belongs to this period. After the fall of Robespierre he was imprisoned, but was released upon the plea of his divorced wife for whom, as a gesture of thanks, he painted the picture *The Sabine Women*. The pair remarried and remained happily together for another thirty years.

With the rise of Napoleon Bonaparte, David became an ardent Bonapartist and between 1802 and 1807 painted a series of pictures glorifying Napoleon's military exploits. The fall of Napoleon sent David into exile in Belgium where he lived until his death in 1825. Unlike Michelangelo, Titian, Rembrandt and others his work did not grow in maturity with increasing age. Instead he reverted to his earlier style but the work no longer had the previous conviction. Much of his more unassuming, yet searching and sensitive, work is to be found in his portraiture and he always remained a considerable colourist and technician.

Death of Marat
(Musées Royaux des Beaux-Arts, Brussels)

This depicts a physically gruesome scene but in a manner which is visually monumental. The empty upper half of the composition is as effective to the subject and the mood of the picture as a funeral pall. Underlying the horror, there is the great tenderness which is the outcome of acute observation and sensitive draughtsmanship by the artist.

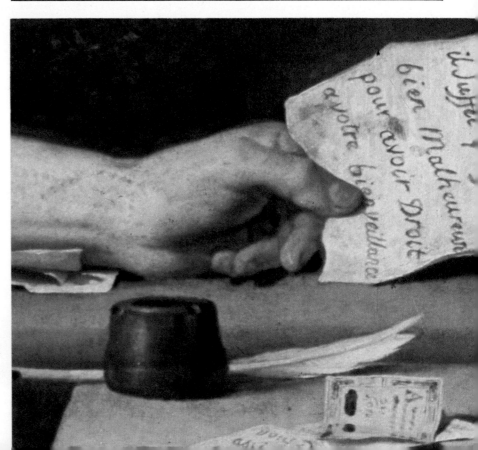

William Blake
1757-1827

William Blake was born in 1757 and was early apprenticed to the engraver, Basire. During his apprenticeship his work led him to a close study of Gothic art, much of it on the spot, in and around Westminster Abbey. It developed in him a love of linear design and of formalised pattern. In 1778 he entered the Royal Academy Schools which merely confirmed in him his distaste for the repetitive dullness of academicism as he saw it. His relations with Sir Joshua Reynolds were far from pleasant although he enjoyed more sympathetic relationships with Flaxman and Fuseli, the latter not being averse to the borrowing of several of Blake's ideas and using them in his own painting.

From about 1787 Blake became absorbed in illustrating in colour his own poems and he produced many volumes including *The Songs of Innocence* of 1789 and the *Songs of Experience* of 1794. Probably his greatest works are the twenty-one illustrations to *The Book of Job,* produced from 1820 and engraved in 1826; the 102 illustrations to Dante; and his colour-printed drawings which include *Nebuchadnezzar* and *Elijah in the Chariot of Fire*. He worked mostly in

water colour, but in his frescoes he used an unorthodox form of tempera which has deteriorated badly with age. He had a prejudice against oil as a medium and experimented widely in different media.

To describe Blake as an individualist is to underestimate him in an almost trivial way. He was poet, philosopher, visionary, engraver as well as painter and it is tempting to compare him with the great figures of the Renaissance, the 'universal men' of such stature and diversity. Perhaps he is best left to speak for himself: 'Any fool can paint the vegetable world, the world of nature; only the artist can paint the world of the imagination.' Blake regarded art, imagination and religion as synonymous and he believed the artist to be engaged in a spiritual activity. At the same time he admired the old masters and his strong interest in, and copying of, the drawings of Michelangelo must have had some bearing on *Elohim creating Adam*.

Blake's work was not widely appreciated in his lifetime and he depended greatly upon the support of his friends. John Linnell, the artist, financed him from about 1818 until the end of his life in 1827. Some of the younger artists, such as John Varley, Edward Calvert and Samuel Palmer admired Blake and his work and regarded themselves as his disciples. His influence has been, and continues to be, powerful and widespread.

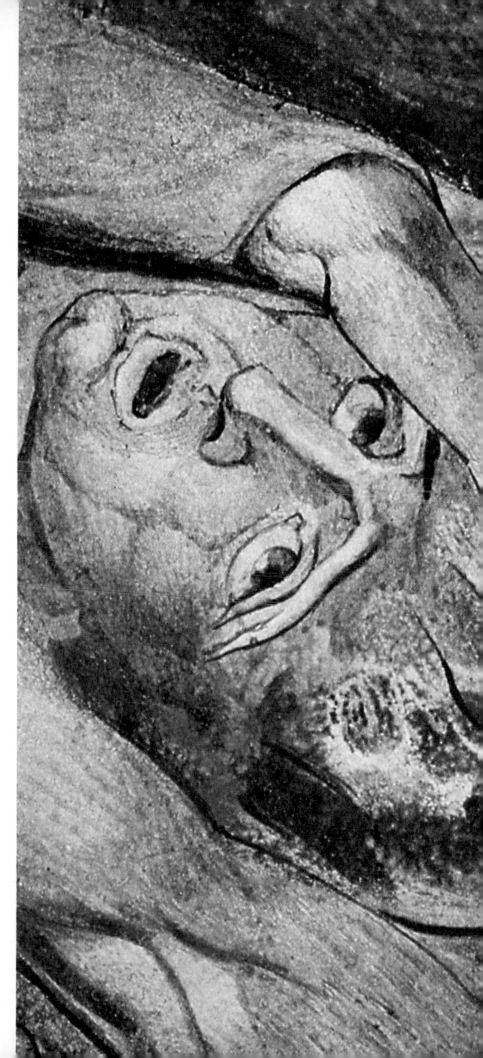

Elohim creating Adam
(Tate Gallery, London)

Comparisons between this picture and Michelangelo's treatment of the subject in the ceiling of the Sistine Chapel in the Vatican are inevitable despite the considerable differences in the two interpretations. The not-quite-touching fingers in the Michelangelo suggest the detachment important to artists of the Classical Renaissance. Blake's Elohim, conversely, moulds his Adam in a much more physically involved and sensuous manner. It is as though Blake himself was the creator which, in the pictorial sense, of course he is. The drawing and the design reflect Blake's influences derived from his study of Gothic art.

Joseph Mallord William Turner 1775-1851

William Turner, son of a barber and wig-maker, showed an early talent for drawing and found employment as a colourist and copyist. He worked, together with Thomas Girtin, for an engraver copying works by artists such as Piranesi and Canaletto. In 1789 he was admitted to the Royal Academy Schools, his first water colours being exhibited in the Academy in 1790 and his first oil painting in 1796. The strongest influence upon his work at this time came from the Dutch marine painters of the 17th century. In 1792 he undertook the

first of his many sketching tours.

The year 1799 saw two significant stages in Turner's development. First, he painted *Norham Castle* which is considered to be his breakthrough into artistic originality. Secondly, he was elected an associate member of the Royal Academy. He was to become a full Academician in 1802, and was appointed Professor of Perspective in the Academy Schools in 1807; he received great support from the Royal Academy throughout the remainder of his life.

During this first decade of the 19th century Turner's painting tended to greater Romanticism but he also spent much time on engraving. Between 1807 and 1809 he produced seventy plates for his book *Liber Studiorum* which was in imitation of Claude's *Liber Veritatis* — a fact which marks his admiration of Claude's work. From 1814 to 1826 he worked on drawings which were published as engravings in Cooke's *Picturesque Views of the Southern Coast of England* and between 1827 and 1830 he was working similarly for the publication *The Ports of England* and for Roger's *Italy*.

It was in 1802 when Turner made his first visit to the continent, ostensibly to see the pictures 'looted' by Napoleon and then on exhibition in Paris. Thereafter he made regular visits to the continent until 1845 and it was his habit on these tours to make rapid sketches of landscape, and atmospheric and light effects for reference use later in imaginative compositions.

He was at the height of his powers in the 1830s and began a transition which was to lead to the more abstract work of the later years. Objects and incidents gave way to atmospheric effects of light and the forces of the elements, and these became the real subject matter of his pictures. His later work was controversial and was attacked by some critics, but was defended by John Ruskin the self-appointed artistic authority in 19th century England.

At his death in 1851 Turner left over three hundred paintings and twenty thousand drawings and watercolours to the nation with the request that they be kept together in one place of permanent exhibition, a wish which has never been fulfilled. He also left a considerable sum of money for the founding of an Artists' Benevolent Fund. This desire was frustrated by the obscurity of his will and by the lawyers who tried to disentangle it.

'The Fighting Téméraire'
tugged to her last Berth to
be broken up
(National Gallery, London)

Painted in 1838, this picture laments the last journey of a brave warship which had distinguished itself at the Battle of Trafalgar. Turner comments on the effects of the industrial revolution. The old, but valiant, ship dissolves into the elemental forces of sunlight, sea and mist to be replaced by the new technology of steam.

John Constable 1776-1837

John Constable was born the son of a rich miller in East Bergholt in Suffolk, England. He showed an early aptitude for drawing landscape and capturing climatic effects in his locality. He was later to say: 'These (Suffolk) scenes made me an artist'. However his powers developed only slowly and in 1795 he was working, not very happily, under Joseph Farington in London.

Constable only committed himself to the artist's life in 1799, at the comparatively late age of 23, when he entered the Royal Academy schools. He was helped and advised by Benjamin West who was known mainly as a painter of historical themes. Constable exhibited in the Royal Academy in 1802 and 1803 but his work made very little impression at the

time. Upon the death of his father in 1816, he became financially secure and soon after married Maria Bicknell. In 1819 he was elected an associate member and in 1829 a full member of the Royal Academy.

The influences which played a part in the early development of Constable came from Gainsborough, Ruisdael, the Dutch 17th-century painters and the English water-colourists. He ranks with Turner as one of the most important painters produced by England in the 19th century. His picture *The Haywain* was exhibited at the Royal Academy in 1820 and represents the beginning of his public recognition as an artist. This picture gained a Gold Medal when exhibited at the Paris Salon of 1824 and

was noted and admired by young French painters, including Géricault and Delacroix.

Constable's large finished pictures, produced for exhibitions at the Royal Academy, were necessary to his acceptance as an artist. His own real interest, though, lay in his 'sketches' and it is these works which have excited the interest of all painters since his death in 1851. It is necessary to clarify the use of the word 'sketch' in this context. These were not rough unfinished works or merely notes. In their free, broad and spontaneous way they were carefully considered and were complete in their pictorial statement. In them, Constable captures the effects of rapidly changing light, showing for example how patterns of light change on a landscape and clouds scud across the sky. They embody his most important contribution to European art and explain why his work made such an impact upon the Impressionists.

> ### Study for 'The Haywain'
> *(Victoria & Albert Museum, London)*
>
> *This is a typical example of a 'sketch' by Constable; its 'finished' counterpart may be seen in the National Gallery in London. The compositional basis of both remains the same, though the details are different as is the precision of depiction. In the sketch, detail and precision are deliberately sacrificed to spontaneity of statement and importance is attached to speed of execution in order to capture changing light and atmospheric effects.*

Jean-Auguste-Dominique Ingres 1780-1867

Ingres was born in Montaubon in south west France. His father was a minor sculptor and painter of miniatures who realised his son's talents and sent him to the Toulouse Academy and then on to Paris in 1796. There he was a fellow student of the painter Gros in the studio of the great Jacques Louis David. In 1801 Ingres won the Prix de Rome but, owing to conditions in France, did not take up his place at the French Academy in Rome until 1807. In the meantime he painted portraits and began to develop the strong and sensuous contour line which remained the basis of his drawing throughout his life.

Ingres stayed in Italy until 1824 during which time his taste for the

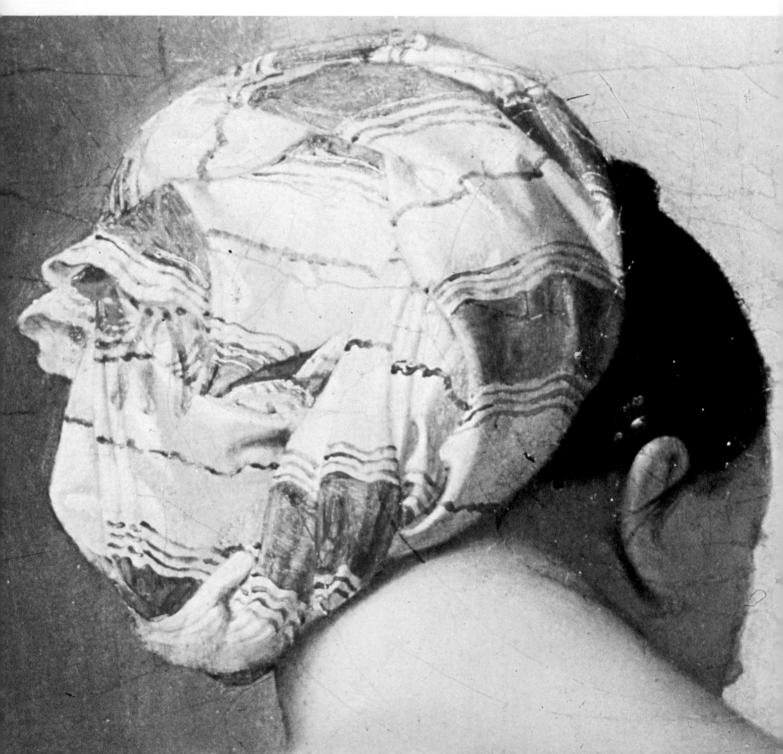

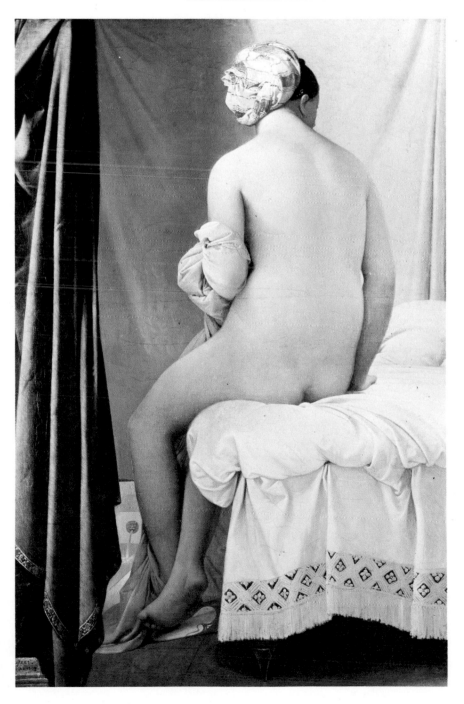

Nude from the Back
(Louvre, Paris)

The containment of the form of the body within the firm but gentle contour lines is clearly seen in this picture. The colour is pleasing but seems subsidiary to the drawing. The compositional design is typically and classically severe.

classical influence became thoroughly established. In that year he returned to France and exhibited *The Vow of Louis XIII* at the Salon. The picture received great acclaim and he was hailed as the leader of the opposition to romantic painting as represented by the work of Géricault and Delacroix. Ingres returned to Rome in 1834 as director of the French Academy and remained in Rome for seven years. When he finally settled in France he became the most generally admired and respected painter in the country. As Professor at the École des Beaux Arts his influence was considerable. In 1855 he was made a Grand Officer of the Legion of Honour and also had a retrospective exhibition of his work at the Exposition Universelle. He was elected a Senator in 1862.

Ingres was intolerant of ideas other than his own and was highly critical of the younger generation of artists. He showed all the artistic limitations of the French middle classes and some of his work was marred by a false sentimentality. His nudes are his greatest works and they express a highly disciplined sensuality. Nude bathers recurred as a constant theme throughout his career. The last, and possibly the greatest, of his pictures on this theme, *The Turkish Bath,* was painted in his eighty-third year in 1862, five years before his death. It is a circular composition, comprising a great number of exquisitely drawn nudes, an astonishing achievement both in composition and in drawing.

It is as a draughtsman that Ingres was supreme. He was a true descendant of Leonardo and the precursor of Degas. He himself said: 'Drawing is the probity [honesty or sincerity] of art, it includes everything except the tint.' Some of his detractors, on the other hand, have unfairly described his painting as merely tinted drawing.

Théodore Géricault 1791-1824

Théodore Géricault was born in Rouen but moved to Paris while still a boy. From 1808 to 1810 he studied with Carle Vernet and then entered the studio of the academic painter Pierre Guérin where Delacroix was subsequently a fellow student. Like most students of his time he made copies from the works of old masters in the Louvre and this developed in him a respect and admiration for the work of Rubens in particular.

Géricault was considerably excited by

Gros' paintings of horses and, fired by Gros, he developed a remarkable technique for painting them which expressively caught their sense of power and movement. At the age of only 21, his picture *The Officer of the Chasseurs Commanding a Charge* was awarded the gold medal at the Salon. Its realistic style was considered by the younger artists of the day as a rejection of the influence of the neo-classical ideas of David.

Between 1816 and 1818 Géricault was mostly in Florence and Rome where he came to admire the work of Michelangelo and the Baroque style. In Paris for a time in 1817, he exhibited *The Raft of the Medusa,* shown below. This depicted an unfortunate event of 1816 which had serious political implications. The *Medusa,* a ship carrying soldiers and settlers to the colony of Senegal, ran aground largely because of the ineptitude of its captain. There were not enough lifeboats so one hundred and

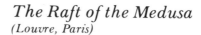

The Raft of the Medusa
(Louvre, Paris)

Géricault incorporates a remarkably powerful pictorial statement with much of the experimentation undertaken by European artists throughout the previous five hundred years. Drawing, movement, colour and light are all exploited to the full to portray a dramatic story with visually dramatic intensity.

fifty people were put on a makeshift raft to be rowed to safety by the lifeboats. The lifeboat crews, in their eagerness to reach the shore, cut the raft adrift. After fifteen days of unspeakable experiences the raft was found with only fifteen people alive. It was a sensitive subject, implying governmental incompetence, and its depiction and exhibition by Géricault was thought inexcusable and aroused strong feeling. Similar strong feeling, coupled with admiration for the picture as a work of art, was expressed when it was shown in England.

Géricault was in England from 1820 to 1822 where he frequented the races and painted them and the jockeys. He also came into contact with the work of Constable and Bonington and his unbounded admiration for their work caused him to introduce it to artists in France upon his return. His preoccupation with horses became obsessive and was almost certainly the cause of his untimely death in 1824, aged only 33. His naturalistic treatment of horses had a strong influence upon the work, later in the century, of Degas and Toulouse-Lautrec.

Eugène Delacroix 1798-1863

Eugène Delacroix's father, Charles Delacroix, took an active part in the Revolution, was Foreign Minister under the Directoire and then Prefect of the Gironde. In 1815 Eugène studied under Pierre Guérin where he met Géricault. However his real training was acquired by copying the works of old masters in the Louvre, particularly those of Rubens, Veronese and the Venetian school. Through Géricault he met the English painter Bonington who introduced him to English water-colour painting. Constable's picture *The*

Haywain impressed and excited him when it was shown at the Salon in 1824 and in the following year, when he spent some time in England, he became enthusiastic about other English painters, such as Gainsborough and Lawrence.

The first Delacroix to be exhibited in the Salon was *Dante and Virgil in Hell* of 1822. This was very well received and was bought by the State. His *Massacre at Chios* and *The Death of Sardanapalus* were exhibited respectively at the Salons of 1823 and 1827. In 1832 he spent some

time in North Africa, an experience which greatly enriched his vocabulary of visual imagery and his use of colour.

From the late 1830s his style changed quite radically. He used the picture surface as a palette, in the divisionist manner, instead of laying on a series of luminous glazes one upon the other. He also applied his paint in a thicker, impasto manner. In 1855 he had thirty-six canvases in the Exposition Universelle and was made a Companion of the Legion of Honour. Despite this success, he was not accepted as a member of the Institute until 1857, though he was now regarded as one of the leaders of the revolt against academic classicism.

Delacroix was always enthusiastic about new ideas and experimental approaches and the Impressionists were greatly influenced by him. At his death in 1863 he left some six thousand drawings and two hundred large paintings. He was a prodigious and energetic worker. He also left a journal which he had kept regularly between 1823 and 1854. It stands as an artistic record of a period of significant developments in European painting, with Paris displacing Italy as the cultural centre.

Liberty leading the People
(Louvre, Paris)

This picture was painted by Delacroix in response to the events of the Revolution in July 1830. It is the only painting in which he used a contemporary political theme since, unlike Géricault and Goya, he was not greatly interested in such matters. The compositional design is direct, simple and effective. All lines of movement and direction lead the eye to the apex of a pyramid which is the head of the woman symbolising France. From that apex the tricolour, symbol of liberty to Frenchmen, waves proudly above the carnage. Colour, drawing and chiaroscuro are all used with great assurance.

Jean-François Millet 1814-1875

Jean-François Millet was born in a small hamlet near Cherbourg, the son of respected and reasonably prosperous peasant farmers. In 1833 he was sent to study with a portrait painter in Cherbourg, returning home frequently to help with work on the farm. Two years later he started full-time studies with a pupil of Gros and this was the year in which he saw the collection of Spanish, Dutch and French paintings which later became the basis of the Museum of Cherbourg.

In 1837 he was given a scholarship by the city of Cherbourg for study in Paris and he enrolled in the studio of Delaroche at the École des Beaux-Arts. His early work consisted of mythological scenes, genre paintings, portraits and some erotic pictures. In 1839 his Cherbourg scholarship was ended and thereafter he had to rely upon his own efforts as a painter to earn a living.

It was in 1848 that Millet's first picture of rustic life, the kind of subject matter now almost exclusively associated with his name, was exhibited at the Salon and met with some praise from the critics. This was *The Winnower*, more sombre in colour and mood than his earlier works, which may reflect the social unrest and revolutionary spirit in Europe in that year.

In 1848 he moved to the village of Barbizon, near Fontainebleau, where he remained for the rest of his life. Several other painters joined him there and together they formed the Barbizon School, devoting themselves entirely to depicting the life and surroundings of the peasants. Millet's picture *The*

The Gleaners
(*Louvre, Paris*)

Colour and mood in this picture are warm and relaxed. In the foreground are the three women gleaning the last ears of corn and in the distance on the left are the stacks, the symbol of a fruitful harvest. On the right lies the village confidently bathed in glorious sunlight. Sky and land, as well as labourers and their work, all seem to be in gentle harmony with each other.

Gleaners was exhibited at the Salon of 1857 and *The Angelus* followed two years later. The latter is probably his most widely known picture, having been reproduced in very large quantities.

Millet left Barbizon briefly in 1870 during the Franco-Prussian war and went to his native district near Cherbourg. In 1871 he refused election as a member of the Fédération des Artistes, newly established by the Commune. By this time his work was in demand and was being regularly exhibited in Paris and London. He was back in Barbizon in 1871 and died there in January 1875.

The work of the Barbizon School is important in its realist insistence upon the pictorial values of the life of the countryman, and in often working directly from observation on site. Millet's own work underlines the serious side of the countryman's life and the toil and labour involved in his survival.

Gustave Courbet
1819-1877

Gustave Courbet was born in Ornans near the Franco-Swiss border. Upon moving to Paris in 1839 to study painting he avoided the official schools apart from sporadic visits to the Atelier Suisse. Most of his study consisted of copying in the Louvre, particularly from the works of Caravaggio and the Spanish painters, Ribera, Zurbaran and Velázquez. With such a diet it is not surprising that his early work was romantic in style and mood.

By 1842 he was firmly fashioning his own strongly realist style. His pictures range from the isolated, heavy manual labourer in *The Stonebreaker* to the depiction of a peasant funeral in *The Burial at Ornans* with its forty life-size figures.

Dissatisfied with the space allotted to him at the Exposition Universelle in 1855, he organised his own exhibition

marquee. At the exhibition of 1867 he showed 110 canvasses under similar conditions, thus defiantly responding to the implied disapproval of his work. He was a man of very independent character and almost obstinate self-confidence. He became a socialist and friend of Zola and of Proudhon, the socialist writer. Courbet was strongly anti-clerical and his picture *The Return from the Conference*, showing drunken priests, was rejected by both the official Salon and the Salon des Réfuses of 1863. It was eventually bought by a devout Catholic who destroyed it.

Courbet was involved in the revolution of 1848 and again in the events of the Commune in 1871. As a result of his part in the destruction of the Vendôme Column in 1871 he was heavily fined and imprisoned, after which he had to leave France for Switzerland where he died in 1877. His last years were spoiled by financial difficulties and by his employing unworthy assistants in the mass production of inferior works.

It was in his choice of subject matter, rather than as a technician, that Courbet was an important innovator and influence. Even so, he did little more than consolidate the realism of Géricault and Delacroix, though his pictures do give a nobility to subjects hitherto considered commonplace and unworthy of artistic attention. Technically, he was competent with a tendency to experiment in unusual media which have not helped his pictures survive the passage of time.

Bonjour M. Courbet
(*Musée Fabré, Montpellier, France*)

This picture shows Courbet in shirtsleeves with haversack and staff, meeting a patron while tramping the countryside. The patron and his friend are well dressed in contemporary clothing. The landscape is faithfully portrayed and very decided shadows are cast by the figures. It is technically very assured and all its elements are deliberately and uncompromisingly stark. Gauguin later painted a 'Bonjour, M. Gauguin' as a homage to Courbet.

William Holman Hunt 1827-1910

William Holman Hunt was a student at the Royal Academy Schools in 1844 where he met John Everett Millais and the painter and poet Dante Gabriel Rossetti. 1848, the year of revolutions throughout Europe, saw another kind of revolt in England. In that year Hunt, Millais and Rossetti formed the Pre-Raphaelite Brotherhood, the first organised revolt against the stranglehold on art and artists exercised by the Royal Academy. More specifically, the revolt

Light of the World
(Keeble College, Oxford)

When dissociated from all the false emotion attached to this picture, it stands as a remarkable achievement of the artist/craftsman's powers. Its compositional design is direct, deliberately simple, and totally appropriate to the artist's purpose of concentrating attention on the figure and its symbolic power. The drawing is convincing in its attention to, and correctness of, detail. The reflected light, both real and artificial, expresses the intensity and drama sought by the artist. A possible artistic weakness is in the sometimes heavy and overworked colour.

was against the pretentious epic or history picture; the trivial anecdotal picture; and what they called the 'monkeyana' of the work of Sir Edwin Landseer, the eminent designer of the lions at the foot of Nelson's Column in Trafalgar Square, London.

It was suggested that the remedy lay in returning to that purity of art which existed before the High Renaissance ('pre-Raphael'). It was also urged by John Ruskin, who wielded immense authority as an art theorist and critic in 19th-century England, that art should re-establish its 'truth to nature'.

The danger in the first aim was that, largely under the influence of Rossetti, they came to look backwards nostalgically, and with false sentiment, to a dreamlike and totally unreal past. In doing so they automatically denied their second aim and the 'truth to nature', as forged by Constable and further explored by so many painters in 19th-century France, became, in their hands, an obsession with mere detail at its most minute and precise. This is not to say that the PRB was not serious and genuine in its aims during the decade of its effective existence as a movement.

Holman Hunt remained quite faithful, in his own estimation, to its aims, ideas and methods and in order to paint *The Scapegoat* of 1854 he literally took goat and painting equipment to the shores of the Dead Sea and painted it on site. Conditions must have been appalling and his endurance and faithfulness to his ideals very great.

Some of Hunt's work, such as *The Light of the World*, is difficult for 20th-century artists to relate to, since its moral and religious connotations do not accord with their experiences and expectations. Hunt was a man of great energy but doubtful taste and his colour, as in the picture *The Hireling Shepherd*, often approached the crude. He lived to the great age of 83, dying in 1910 in what must have appeared to him a strange and alien world.

Edouard Manet 1832-1883

Edouard Manet was born the son of a well-to-do middle-class family. His father was reluctant to let him embark upon the precarious and dubious career of artist but, in 1850, Manet was permitted to enrol in the studio of Couture where he remained until 1856.

The evolution of his style was not based, however, on the classical academic teaching he received, but on his studies of the old masters in the Louvre. He was particularly influenced by the Spanish painters, Velázquez, Murillo and Ribera. After leaving the studio of Couture he travelled widely in Europe but, strangely, not in Spain where he could have seen more of the works of the artists whom he so admired.

Manet's *Absinthe Drinker,* with its reference to the seamier side of life, was rejected by the Salon in 1859. In 1861 two of his paintings were accepted but *Déjeuner sur l'Herbe* caused an uproar when shown at the Salon des Réfuses in 1863. The Emperor Napoleon III caused the picture to be removed and the exhibition closed. Such public reaction now seems strange since, by basing his work on the picture *Concert Champêtre* by the highly respected old master, Giorgione, Manet was expressing his respect for the inherited tradition of European art. The trouble seems to have arisen from his depiction of a nude woman seated between two men clothed in contemporary 19th-century dress. Two years later his picture *Olympia* was again considered scandalous but this

Un Bar aux Folies Bergères
(Courtauld Institute, London)

The compositional design of this picture is both splendidly simple and subtle. The lateral lines of the counter, its reflection in the mirror, and the line of people are broken by the upright of the girl and her reflection. It is this upright, and those of the bottles, which hold the design together. The foreground still-life groups on either side of the girl each represent a picture in themselves, at the same time as belonging to the overall design. The colour is a sensual delight and its handling is masterly.

time it did receive the support of influential men like Zola and Baudelaire.

The younger generation of artists began to regard him as a master, but he continued to seek the support of the official Salon and he regarded himself as a gentleman-artist, not as a Bohemian. He was influenced by, and worked with, the Impressionists but always held himself somewhat aloof from them. In the 1870s, urged on by Berthe Morisot and Monet, he did adopt the practice of working out of doors and was converted to the use of divisionist technique and the rainbow palette evolved by Renoir. That he was essentially a realist, opposed to romantic ideas, and painted the world as he saw it with objectivity is made clear in *Un Bar aux Folies Bergères*.

Towards the end of his life he received some official recognition. He was elected to the Legion of Honour and, by the time of his death in 1883, many of the ideas which he had adapted from Impressionism were affecting even academic art.

Edgar Degas 1834-1917

Edgar Degas was born in Paris, the son of a wealthy family. He abandoned a training for the law and entered the École des Beaux-Arts in 1855 where he worked under Lamothe, an ex-pupil and admirer of Ingres. This laid the foundations of Degas' exceptional powers of draughtsmanship and his own admiration for Ingres. In 1856 he joined his family, then living in Naples, and visited other Italian cities, spending three years in Rome where he copied frescoes by Italian artists of the 15th and 16th centuries. He returned to Paris in 1861, worked very much in the manner of Ingres and seemed to be firmly set on the course of an academic painter, but, in that same year, he met Manet when they were both copying in the Louvre.

Through this contact, Degas was introduced to the Impressionists and he changed his approach to his work. In 1862 he painted his first racecourse picture, and thereafter his pictures were always of realistic contemporary scenes, particularly of the ballet, circus and cafés. He exhibited in seven of the eight Impressionist exhibitions but was never wholly committed to Impressionism and, like Manet, stood aloof from the group and some of its ideas. He was not interested in painting landscapes, nor was he so interested in the changing effects of light — and he had no interest in working out of doors. But, like the Impressionists, he used the spontaneous effect of figures cut off at the edges of a composition and was stimulated by the developments in photography and by the Japanese prints then being seen in Europe for the first time.

His own inclination, his thorough grounding in traditional techniques, and his knowledge of the Italian Renaissance combined to give his work an individualistic approach strongly based upon his draughtsmanship. He had always used pastel a great deal and from the 1880s, as his sight began to fail, he increased his use of this medium. His colour became stronger and his compositional designs simpler. He began to model in wax and produced some seventy such sculptures, many of which have since been cast in bronze. His last years were marred by his increasing blindness but, by his death in 1917, he had achieved recognition and fame and that fame has endured and grown.

L'Absinthe
(Louvre, Paris)

The realism of this picture is so poignant as to make it a picture of 'mood'. The brilliant colour and the light centred on the woman and glass are dramatically offset by the dark and threatening shapes of the man and the cast shadows. The non-symmetrical composition is tautly handled and the economy of drawing makes the picture deceptively casual.

Paul Cézanne
1839-1906

Paul Cézanne, the son of a prosperous banker in Aix-en-Provence, was born in 1839. Emile Zola, the realist writer, was a close school friend. Their friendship lasted for nearly fifty years and was broken only by the publication of Zola's book *L'Oeuvre* in which the character, Claude Lantier, seemed to be rather unkindly based upon Cézanne himself.

It was Zola who persuaded Cézanne to abandon his law studies and to study painting in Paris, where he was introduced to Courbet and Manet and very soon met the Impressionist group.

Mont Sainte-Victoire
(Metropolitan Museum of Art, New York)

This is one of the many pictures of the hill which overlooks Cézanne's home town of Aix-en-Provence. The design is separated into three clear areas: the foreground of trees and housetop; the middle distance marked particularly by the viaduct; and the farther distance of hills and sky. This is achieved by modulating the colour in the traditional way, but Cézanne also uses his newly evolved manner of laying on the brush stroke so that it describes the geometrical form he saw in all nature. He does not wish to abandon spatial relationships and recession in painting, but this picture has more two-dimensional feeling than had become usual in the painting of the previous four centuries.

But his chief mentor at that time was Delacroix and his own work then consisted of romantic themes of a somewhat violent nature. In the 1860s he began to adopt some of the methods of the Impressionists, painting direct from nature and with greater self-discipline. He started a long working association with Camille Pissarro in 1872 and, at the end of his life, described himself as a 'pupil of Pissarro'.

Cézanne exhibited with the Impressionists in 1874 and 1877 but he never felt able wholly to identify himself with them. He was not primarily interested in realism, fleeting impressions or light effects. He wished to mould the ideas of the Impressionists into something as solid and enduring as the work of the Renaissance masters.

Cézanne's father died in 1886, leaving him a rich man. He returned to Provence and lived out the remainder of his life there in comparative seclusion, painting constantly and developing his artistic ideas gradually and almost painfully. The picture *Mont Sainte-Victoire,* shown opposite, is one of the very many of this subject that he worked on laboriously and carefully over many years. The hill overlooks his home town of Aix and the road he took to make his studies of it is now called 'Route de Cézanne'.

In 1895 he had an exhibition at the gallery of Ambroise Vollard and, from this time on, he was regarded as a master and innovator by the younger artists. He had abandoned a portrait of Vollard after more than a hundred sittings with the comment that he was 'not dissatisfied with the shirt front'.

Cézanne died in 1906 and continues to exert a profound influence upon painters and painting. His ideas and aims are still only imperfectly understood and further comprehension will occupy and stimulate many generations of painters to come.

Claude Monet 1840-1926

Claude Monet was born in Paris but went to live in Le Havre as a boy and it was there that, in his teens, he met the marine painter Boudin who urged the young Monet to start landscape painting. He was in Paris in 1859, studying at the Atelier Suisse, where Courbet had been before him, and there he formed a close friendship with Camille Pissarro.

After two years military service in Algiers between 1860 and 1862 he made a brief visit to Le Havre. On this occasion he met another marine painter, Jongkind, and his interest in landscape painting was confirmed. On his return to Paris in 1862, he worked for a time in Gleyre's studio where he met Renoir, Sisley and Bazille. This was followed by a time painting in Barbizon where he met Millet and other members of the Barbizon School. In 1865, he was working in Trouville with the admired and controversial Courbet.

All these contacts helped to forge the direction in which Monet was to develop. He did not study and make copies of old masters in the Louvre. He was largely self-taught but highly receptive to both the ideas and techniques of his contemporaries and his work in 1866, for example, possesses a

bright clarity of light and colour which reflects his contact with Manet at that time. The development of his style went on throughout his long life but its basis, and his leadership of the Impressionist group, was established by the 1870s. The emphasis was on the importance of light as the describer of objects and events and, therefore, upon light as the real subject matter of the picture. Painting was done on site, out of doors, at all times of day, so that all effects of light could be studied and translated into paint.

Monet's last years were spent painting virtually one subject, his own garden, which he had gradually transformed into a series of lily ponds. The reflective water, the vegetation and the light and atmospheric effects were enough to occupy his attention and efforts for the rest of his life. His later very large

pictures became almost abstract relationships of colour and light. He died in 1926 and Cézanne's words serve as an effective epitath: 'He was only an eye but, my God, what an eye'.

Impression: Sunrise
(Musée Marmottan, Paris)

This was the picture from which the group label was born in 1872. A critic dismissed the picture as 'merely an impression' and Monet and his friends thereafter proudly called themselves Impressionists. Even this early picture has strong abstract, non-representational qualities. The incidents of boat, figure, water, sky and sun are all softly and gently implied rather than clearly stated and this very fact is what welds them all together. What is stated as fact is the effect of light and atmospherics and mist over water at sunrise.

Pierre-Auguste Renoir 1841-1919

Pierre-Auguste Renoir was born in Limoges in 1841 but the family moved to Paris in 1845 and, by the age of thirteen, he was working as a painter in a porcelain factory, an experience which had a lasting effect upon his use of colour. In 1862 he became a student in Gleyre's studio and there formed close and lasting friendships with Monet, Sisley and Bazille. He painted with them in Barbizon; became for a time a leading member of the Impressionist group in its discussions in the Café Guerbois; and exhibited in four of the eight Impressionist exhibitions.

In the 1880s Renoir began to withdraw from the Impressionists and to develop the highly individualistic ideas

Gabrielle with Rose
(Louvre, Paris)

This is a particularly beautiful example of the work of his later years. Gabrielle came as a servant and model to the Renoir household in 1894 and stayed many years, being frequently painted by Renoir. This picture dates from 1911 and its outstanding features are simplicity of composition; the almost sculptural quality of the painted figure; and the sensuous yet delicately controlled pearly quality of the colour.

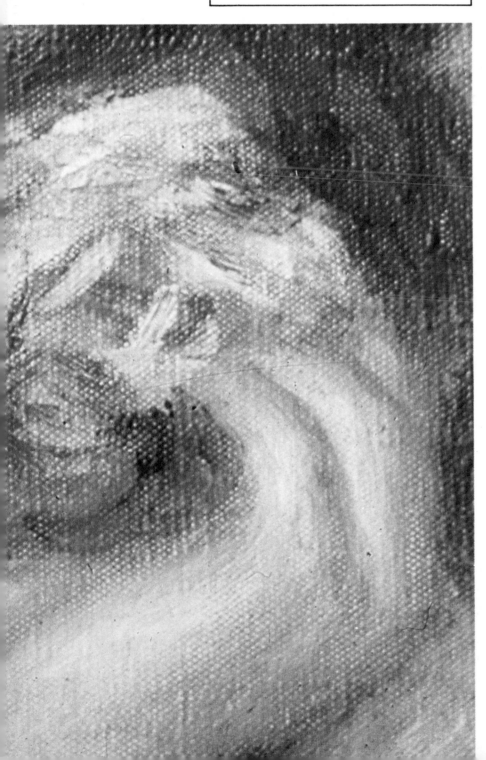

and techniques of his maturity. A highly successful exhibition of his work at the Durand-Ruel Gallery in Paris in 1883 confirmed him in his new direction and, from this time, his work became more classical in feeling and form. Between 1904 and his death he lived in Provence, now quite famous and with his work selling well. He was increasingly crippled by rheumatoid arthritis but continued to paint with the aid of specially long brushes which were strapped to his fingers, wrist and just below the elbow.

Renoir's technical contribution falls into two parts. He introduced the 'rainbow palette' by which pure tones of maximum intensity are employed and black is not used at all. He also insisted upon a more thoroughly consistent use of divisionism as expounded by Watteau in the previous century, by which pure colours are applied directly to the canvas and their mingling is left to the eye of the spectator.

The human figure plays a large part in Renoir's painting and in his latter years in Provence he produced the great female nudes, great both in conception and in size. He delighted in the charm of children, lovely women, flowers and beautiful landscapes. His landscapes have no hint of melancholy or dark mystery; they are open and vibrant with brilliant light. He consistently sought to combine in his paintings the loveliness which he saw in mankind and nature with sensuality of colour and pigment. In his later years in Provence he experimented in media other than paint and became very interested in exploring the third dimension by working in modelled sculpture.

In addition to his admiration for Watteau, Renoir thought highly of the work of Fragonard and, as he himself developed in maturity of outlook and style, he was increasingly affected by the work of Titian, Rubens and van Dyck. It is interesting to reflect that Renoir lived far into this century and that many of his late works have semi-abstract qualities which foreshadow the experiments of abstract painters later in the century.

Henri Rousseau 1844-1910

Henri Rousseau, known as Douanier Rousseau, was born in 1844 and, at the age of 18, did his military service as a saxophonist in a military band. He claimed to have served in Mexico when the French army was involved in the attempt to install the Hapsburg Maximilian as Emperor of Mexico and it has been thought that this early experience might explain the tropical vegetation which recurs in many of his paintings. The claim cannot, however, be substantiated with any certainty. In 1866 he took up a minor post in the Customs & Excise Service and hence his nickname of 'le Douanier'.

It was not until about 1884 that he started to paint as a part-time hobby which was aimed at supplementing his pension upon retirement. In 1886 he was introduced by Paul Signac, a follower of Seurat, to the Société des Artistes Indépendants and exhibited in their salon regularly from that time. Rousseau also made contact with Gauguin, Pissarro and Seurat who were all very interested in his work, and it was particularly admired by Renoir, Odilon Redon and Toulouse-Lautrec. The respect shown by this wide variety of people demonstrates recognition of its intrinsic quality of directness, sincerity and personal conviction.

Rousseau was quite untaught, both technically and in the traditions of western European art. He was naive and ingenuous and is usually labelled as a 'primitive', which is inadequate as a description of either the man or his work. The fantasy in some of his work as, for example, in *The Dream,* has a quality of sophistication which was quickly appreciated by the Surrealists in this century. It is impossible to fit Rousseau into a convenient niche and, curiously enough, his highest ambition was to paint in the academic way.

Rousseau's work aroused the interest of Picasso in 1905 and he is recorded as having said to Picasso: 'We are the two greatest artists of our day; you in the Egyptian manner, I in the modern.' He may have been right; certainly his work has aroused great and continuing interest and has had wide-ranging effect. He died alone in 1910, the year in which he painted *The Dream,* and was buried in a pauper's grave.

Tropical Storm with a Tiger
(National Gallery, London)

A delightful example of Rousseau's painting of the tropical vegetation he claimed to have known in Mexico. It is equally delightful in its colour and the element of fantasy which makes his work so beloved of the Surrealists.

Paul Gauguin
1848-1903

Paul Gauguin was born the son of a journalist from Orléans. His mother was a Creole and most of his childhood was spent with her in Peru. Between 1865 and 1871 he was a merchant sailor and then became a successful stockbroker in 1872. He had dabbled in paint from an early age, was now a 'Sunday painter' and bought paintings, including some by Cézanne, whose importance he recognised even then. In 1874 he met Camille Pissarro, through whom he saw the first Impressionist exhibition. He himself exhibited in the fifth and last three Impressionist exhibitions. At this time he was married and, apparently, settled in his career. However, in 1883 he took the hazardous step of changing from being a 'Sunday painter' to a full time professional artist. The move was not supported by his wife and relationships between them were very strained thereafter.

In 1886 Gauguin left Paris and moved to Brittany where he became the focus of a group of younger painters attracted by his ideas and his charismatic personality. From this time he firmly broke with Impressionist ideas and techniques. He was concerned to free colour from a merely representational function and to use it for decorative and emotional purposes. He became more interested, too, in the rhythms of line and shape and the unavoidable two-dimensionality of the picture surface. In doing so he

pointed a way forward to 20th-century abstract painting. Other aspects of his work are akin to the approach of the Surrealists who certainly add his name to their Pantheon of forerunners. He gave the title 'Synthetism' to his aims at that time, claiming that his pictures were a synthesis of visual experiences, emotional reactions, and the demands of pictorial design.

After a brief and disastrous period with van Gogh in Arles, Gauguin, totally disenchanted with western civilisation, left Europe for the South Pacific in 1891. Apart from brief returns to Paris, to settle family matters and raise much needed money, he remained in the South Pacific for the rest of his life. His greatest paintings were produced there and he died there in 1903, leaving a legacy of influence upon art and artists.

Nevermore
(Courtauld Institute, London)

This picture is typical of the paintings which Gauguin produced during his time in the South Pacific. The colour is varied and rich, with dramatic contrasts as in the vermilion above the feet and the yellow pillow. The compositional design gives a satisfying sense of harmony and balance. Close inspection arouses curiosity about the implied mysteries. What, who, and why are the two figures in secret conclave behind the couch; what is the significance of the black bird of omen; and why the wary look in the eyes of the reclining figure?

Vincent van Gogh 1853-1890

Vincent van Gogh was the son of a Protestant Pastor. At the age of 16 he was working in the Dutch branch of Goupil Galleries and in 1873 was sent to work in the London branch. An unsuccessful love affair with his landlord's daughter disturbed what proved to be his precarious emotional stability. He was moved to Paris in 1875, became increasingly sensitive to the social inequalities around him, and abandoned his career as an art dealer, dismissing it as an irrelevant luxury.

After several unsuccessful attempts to become a missionary, he was sent to work as a lay-preacher among the poor miners of the Borinage in southern Belgium. He exercised extreme self-sacrifice in his anxiety to identify with the people among whom he was working and this brought another breakdown; he was forced to relinquish his work.

In 1881, van Gogh returned to Holland determined to become an artist, a determination which reflected the same concentrated energy as he had shown in the Borinage. He was almost entirely self-taught, although he did receive some help from his cousin, the painter Antoine Mauve, and he studied technique for a short time at the Antwerp Academy. He drew incessantly and his observational powers became ever more sensitive and acute. His picture *The Potato-Eaters* is probably the best of his works from this early period.

Van Gogh returned to Paris in 1886 where he quickly came into contact with the Impressionists whose work made an enormous impact upon him, especially upon his use of colour. In search of more colour he moved south to the stronger sun of Provence in 1888. In the fifteen months he spent in Arles he produced more than two hundred canvasses and this is the period of his mature work. His work is called 'Expressionist' which implies the most subjective and emotional approach by a painter. He attached emotional values to colours: blues and yellows represented happiness; red and greens 'those evil things', men's passions. His early period in Arles was a happy one and this is reflected in the colours used in such paintings as *The Chair and The Pipe*.

An attempt at starting an artists' colony in Arles with Gauguin ended in van Gogh attacking the much stronger Gauguin after a series of disagreements. This resulted in a kind of brainstorm, after which he cut off part of his own ear and then sought voluntary admission to the mental hospital at St. Rémy. He was encouraged to continue painting and in the year he spent in the hospital he produced much work, including the famous *Yellow Cornfield*. He left the hospital to stay with Dr Gachet, a patron of painters, living in Auvers-sur-Oise where he was found dead of a self-inflicted bullet wound in the woods nearby.

It is salutary to remember that van Gogh's vast output was produced in ten years, between the ages of 28 and 38; that the most widely known and loved painter in the 20th century never sold a picture in his lifetime; and that his influence has been, and will probably continue to be, incalculable.

The Chair and The Pipe
(Tate Gallery, London)

The yellows and blues representing happiness are predominant in this picture, and the reds of the floor tiles, with their threat of 'those evil passions', are modified with blues and yellows. The subject matter is simple in the extreme and highly unusual for its time; prevailing taste would have found difficulty in seeing any artistic significance in a picture of a humble chair and pipe. The design is masterly in its economic simplicity and the handling of the colour has a tactile quality which is almost sculptural.

Georges Seurat
1859-1891

Georges Seurat first studied under Henri Lehmann, an academic artist and ex-pupil of Ingres, at the École des Beaux-Arts in Paris. Seurat came to share his teacher's admiration for Ingres but, between 1876 and 1884, he experimented in many different ways. He studied the paintings of Delacroix in the church of St. Sulpice in Paris and also those of the Barbizon School and of the Impressionists. He also studied Chevreul's book on colour theory and became interested in the optical and colour researches of the scientists Charles Henry and David Sutter.

His reading and his own practical experiments led him to recall the divisionism first practised by Watteau in the 20th century. The technique of painting which he evolved he termed 'optical painting' and he declared his aims as threefold: first, to apply the principles of divisionism in as exact and scientific a way as possible; second, to achieve the highest degree of luminosity and brilliance of colour; and third, to make of Impressionism something more classical and less romantic, something more scientific and less accidental.

Seurat's method has since come to be known as 'pointillism', a term which is largely self-explanatory. The colour was applied in dabs or points of pure colour and an area of green grass would be suggested by dabs of blue and yellow, the proportion of each colour varying according to the blueness or yellowness of the grass as it reflected different intensities of light in different areas. His most widely known picture, *Un*

Dimanche à la Grande Jatte, which clearly demonstrates his technique, was first shown at the last Impressionist Exhibition in 1886. Despite its exhibition there, its painter made a significant contribution to the breakaway from Impressionism. His work is sometimes described as Neo-Impressionist, but he is often referred to as the first of the Post-Impressionists.

Seurat died in 1891, aged only 32 and, although speculation is fruitless, it is intriguing to wonder how his attempt to apply scientific principles more rigidly to pictorial art would have developed had he lived to a greater age. He had a few 'followers' but none who took the fundamentals of his ideas any further, nor has there been any serious attempt to do so since his time.

Un Dimanche à la Grande Jatte
(Art Institute of Chicago, Helen Birch Bartlett Foundation)

This very large composition is considered to be Seurat's finest achievement and is also thought to be a precise demonstration of his ideas and technique. The finished picture was only arrived at after many studies. Its classical composition underlines Seurat's rejection of Impressionism and the immobilising of activity emphasizes his severe classical approach.

Pablo Picasso 1881-1973

Pablo Picasso was born in 1881. the son of a drawing master in Malaga, Spain. He studied in Corunna and Barcelona before going to Paris in 1900 and the strongest and most obvious influence in his work at that time came from Toulouse-Lautrec. Between 1902 and 1903 he produced the work of his 'Blue' period which was followed by the 'Rose' period of 1905 to 1907 and the 'Negro' period of 1907 to 1909.

In 1906/7 he painted the picture *Les Demoiselles d'Avignon* which marks the first major turning point in his work. It was not understood by the bulk of his contemporary painters and was not exhibited until 1937. It represented the beginning of 'Cubism', probably the most intellectual art style yet attempted.

Picasso worked in close collaboration on the development of the ideas of Cubism first with Georges Braque and later with Juan Gris. The first period was severely classical in composition. The range of colour used was so limited as to be virtually monochromatic; it is referred to as 'High Analytical Cubism'. The second phase, which introduced more colour and the use of collage, is called 'Synthetic Cubism', but the ideas of Cubism remain vague and the pronouncements of Picasso, Braque and Gris are often contradictory.

In 1917 Picasso worked with Jean Cocteau designing scenery and costumes for ballet. Throughout the 1920s his work was increasingly concerned with the story of the Minotaur from Ancient Crete and other classical themes. In the 1930s his attention switched to themes of weeping women and dying horses. The Civil War in Spain disturbed him greatly and he produced his great *Guernica* in response to the bombing of the town of that name, for exhibition in the Spanish Pavilion at the Exposition Universelle in Paris in 1937. This picture marks Picasso's second major turning point and it ranks with Goya's *3 May 1808* in its pictorial reaction to the horrors of war.

Picasso remained in France throughout World War II, partly in Paris and partly in the south. In 1946 he worked in the pottery town of Vallauris on ceramic sculpture and, during the 1950s, he produced two large series of works based on Delacroix's painting *Women of Algiers* and Velázquez' *Las Meninas*. He continued to work ceaselessly right up to his death in 1973.

The personality of this man, his dynamic energy and his diversity of experimentation and innovation in so many different media has dominated the development of the visual arts in this century. His technical brilliance and his imaginative powers rank him among the highest in the history of western European art, to whose traditions he remained, in all fundamental senses, true.

The Three Dancers
(Tate Gallery, London)

This picture represents almost as significant a point in Picasso's development as Les Demoiselles d'Avignon *of 1907 which led to the experiments of Cubism. It comes after his experiences in theatre design and his visit to Italy which reawakened his interest in classical art. There are echoes of the emphases made by the Surrealists but it foreshadows the psychologically and emotionally disturbing qualities of his next phase which culminated in the great* Guernica.

125